And It Is So

The Power of His Promise

Jaculin H. Jones

Order this book online at www.trafford.com
or email orders@trafford.com

Most Trafford titles are also available at major online book retailers.

Scripture quotations marked KJV are from the Holy Bible, King James Version (Authorized Version). First published in 1611. Quoted from the KJV Classic Reference Bible, Copyright © 1983 by The Zondervan Corporation.

Print information available on the last page.

ISBN: 978-1-4907-9374-0 (sc)
ISBN: 978-1-4907-9373-3 (e)

Library of Congress Control Number: 2019935458

Our mission is to efficiently provide the world's finest, most comprehensive book publishing service, enabling every author to experience success. To find out how to publish your book, your way, and have it available worldwide, visit us online at www.trafford.com

Any people depicted in stock imagery provided by Getty Images are models, and such images are being used for illustrative purposes only.
Certain stock imagery © Getty Images.

Trafford rev. 04/23/2019

www.trafford.com
North America & international
toll-free: 1 888 232 4444 (USA & Canada)
fax: 812 355 4082

Acknowledgements

Lord, let my lips always speak of your great goodness and utter your praise.

I dedicate this writing to my husband, Clarence Jones Jr., who loves me like Christ loves the church and gave Himself for it. Thank you for never leaving my side and for upholding our vows for better or for worse. Thank you for walking with me and giving me the courage to write just a portion of our story.
You are my one and only!

To my daughter, Avery, thank you for putting me to task regarding my music and this writing. What a role reversal as I've taught you to finish what you start! Your encouragement means so much to me. Thank you for your creativity in making this book beautiful from the outside in. You too have a voice in this world to share God's goodness through your work. I know you'll do just that. I love you so much.

To my son, Clarence III, only you can tell your story, so the totality of our journey is waiting for you to write. But, I thank God for the miracle He continues to work in your life. You beat the odds of what the world would have considered hopeless. You have strengthened me in ways I never could have imagined. Continue to pursue God. He has His hand on you. I love you so much.

To all of my sisters, brothers, in loves, family and friends too numerous to name, I want to personally thank you for keeping your lips close to God's ear. He heard you and I am here today because the prayers of the righteous availed much.
For this I am eternally grateful.

Contents

Forward

I am honored to write the foreword for this manuscript. As the oldest of the bunch I have had a front row seat to many of the most important events in Jaculin's life. Not only have I been an eye witness, but I have also been an active participant. Jaculin and I have shared our hopes, dreams, aspirations, disappointments, and shed many tears. But, more importantly, we have shared a multitude of joy, laughter, and triumphs.

Reflecting on Jaculin's journey, I'm reminded of Deuteronomy 11:19 (KJV). It reads, *"And ye shall teach them your children, speaking of them when thou sittest in thine house, and when thou walkest by the way, when thou liest down, and when thou risest up."* That about sums up growing up as Joe, and Nita's kids. Juanita's spiritual instruction began in the womb. We had praying parents who taught us how to pray and the power of prayer. They were always interceding on behalf of their children. To God be the Glory!

I thank God for giving Jaculin the inspiration to share her journey with you. This book will take you on an abbreviated journey because there is so much more to be shared by this Awesome Woman of God. Turn the pages expecting to be blessed by Jaculin's ups, downs, her setbacks, and challenges but more assuredly her victories through Jesus Christ. Be encouraged as you read in her words of how God took her through life-threatening and life-altering events, and the people he so carefully selected and placed in her life to minister to her throughout her time of need. I hope that you will be inspired, encouraged, and challenged to trust God throughout all of your experiences.

I love you, Hannah. I pray that your words will be a blessing to all who read this memoir and that you will continue to be blessed as you boldly proclaim who God is and what He continues to do in your life. Remain steadfast in your faith using your many talents to bring honor and glory to the Lord. Continue to let your light shine to demonstrate how worthy He is of all of our praises.

Rosemary Leonard-Bethea

A Note from the Author

I performed in a play as a world-renowned author and recited an excerpt from an imaginary book I was promoting entitled "And It Is So." Wouldn't you know after the play a woman so moved by the words wanted to know where she could buy the book. There was no book, but the conversation with God was real; as real as the family crisis we were experiencing. The exchange that evening followed by the life-threatening events that came to claim my very life, leave me with the responsibility to let the world know what the Lord has done and that He is no respect of person. This book is a forever reminder that God keeps His promises along this journey we call life.

Life is like each flower's bloom. It starts as a seed, and in time transforms, stretching toward the sky to unveil its beauty. It depicts a seemingly effortless journey. Yet, it's journey through the dirt and elements in the atmosphere make it vulnerable to seen and unseen forces that might otherwise impede its growth. Miraculously, though, life's purpose prevails.

I liken this to the sovereignty of God whose purpose for my life was greater than my experiences. My faith has increased as a result and I'm growing to believe God for the impossible. I don't know if this would have been realized if it hadn't been for these afflictions. Though the victories have not been without tears and scars, I can now attest to the lyrics in my mother's favorite song, "Through It All." "Through it all, I've learned to trust in Jesus, I've learned to trust in God." I'm still learning.

I pray as you walk through this miraculous journey with me that you will be encouraged to believe with every confidence that God keeps His promises on earth as they are in heaven. There's no place you can go that He's not there and no state so low that He can't lift you up. He did it for me. I'm a mercy case; a living miracle and testament of God's grace. I don't deserve His goodness, and I've done nothing to gain His favor, but it is by His sovereign will that I am not consumed and for that I am eternally grateful.

Such things were written in the Scriptures long ago to teach us. And the Scriptures give us hope and encouragement as we wait patiently for God's promises to be fulfilled.

Romans 15:4

Sunshine and Cloudy Days

Still, in the womb the ninth of ten children, how did she do it? I lived with superwoman, and I didn't really appreciate it growing up as most children don't. Mommy told me while she was carrying me in her womb there was an explosion in the kitchen of our home. My oldest brother Joseph (Jody) was burned severely. I'm sure the stress of that ordeal took a toll on her body because she said she was having seizures at the time of my birth. I, of course, couldn't have arrived at a worst time, but God blessed her with a healthy baby girl. I know she prayed and I'm sure her hands were full taking care of my brother. So, the responsibility of taking care of my other seven siblings and I fell to my oldest sister Rosemary. I actually thought she was my mother until after she left for college. She taught me a lot about life and demonstrated the importance of getting an education. She set the standard and was the first in our immediate family to go to college. Well as for me, a whole lot of crazy happened while I was in college. I'd often tell my good girlfriends God had His hands on me, but His eyes were closed. It was hard to believe that my sins weren't greater than His love. I was a mess and worthy of death, but He loved me so much and had a purpose for my life that I couldn't have known at the time. Prayerfully and thankfully I graduated from Trenton State College, now known as The College of New Jersey and acquired a pretty nice job.

In addition to receiving my degree, one of the best things that came out of my college experience was a friendship I forged with a really nice young man named Clarence Jones Jr. He was on a mission to finish his degree, and by the time we became friends I was serious about my own future. I learned that he liked French Apple Pie, so I would surprise him every now and then. He was also very kind to me and would periodically allow me to borrow his car to go to work. We were just really good friends. He finished college before me, but not without me. We started dating after he graduated, continued a long-distance relationship and a few years later he decided to come back to get his "good thing."

Me and Mr. Jones wed in the summer of 1988. We decided, or maybe I decided before getting married, that I would continue working in New Jersey after our honeymoon and come to my new home in Maryland on the weekends. Well, that lasted every bit of a month. He returned to get me and the last of my belongings, and that was when our life as husband and wife really began. I slowly adjusted to my new life in Maryland. I enjoyed married life, but I also missed my family back home and going to church. By no means was I living above the clouds singing hallelujah like a deep old seasoned saint, but I understood the importance of a church home for the spiritual growth of my family. Growing up in a family with ten siblings, dealing with our own family dysfunction, disappointments and feelings of abandonment, the one constant was church. My mother saw to it, so it would be no different for my family.

Clarence Jr. and I visited a few churches of family and friends, but none seemed to be the right place for us until a divine encounter with a friend named Melissa. She was also from New Jersey and had been living in the area for some time. We ran into each other during an interview for the same job in Washington, D.C. God knows how happy I was to see a familiar face. She told me she attended the Refreshing Spring Church of God in Christ and extended an invitation. Well, that was music to my ears. I planned to go the next Sunday by myself. Yes, by myself. I wanted to check this one out before I brought Clarence Jr. into the kind of church I grew up in. In some way, I wanted to protect him. It's funny now how I so enjoy hearing him say, "Who-da known!" I guess that's his way of expressing how far he's come in his own faith journey.

I sat in the back of the church that Sunday enjoying the opening hymn sung by the choir, followed by the break out contemporary gospel singing and then the fire filled preaching by Pastor Bishop Archie D. Headen. I could feel the presence of God in that place. It felt like home. The next Sunday, Clarence Jr. and I went to church together. I could tell the high praise, and the marathon dancing unto the Lord was new to him, but in his usual fashion, he sat observing quietly. On our way to church after attending a few Sundays, I told him I wanted to become a member of the church. I said I would wait to give my family time to come and share in what would have been a special occasion, but you wouldn't believe what happened. That very same Sunday, as Pastor Headen opened the doors of the church before I knew anything I was propelled out of my seat and down at the alter taking the right hand of fellowship! I can't explain what happened, but I knew it had to be God. Clarence Jr., on the other hand, didn't know what happened. I could hear him thinking, "What?" Let's just say he was quiet for the remainder of the week. His new bride was making a few decisions on her own, but it wasn't me. This was God. I'm sure he thought the same thing when the spirit fell on me one Sunday just before the benediction. I found myself dancing in the center aisle.

In the early '90s, we were blessed with two children; our first-born was Ms. Avery. We enjoyed every ounce of her. She was just a beautiful, little feisty girl who filled our lives with so much joy. I wasn't sure if I had enough love left for another child, but God blessed us three years later with Mr. Clarence III. We loved our little man just the same. We had to reel him in from time to time, but his daddy was time enough for both of them. He'd tell them then as he still does today, "There's a method to my madness," always creating teachable moments whether they liked it or not.

Their high school years, often the drama years for most parents, were the most enjoyable. We kept the children close to us, while they kept us busy with extra-curricular and church activities. Avery was a well-rounded student who involved herself in every activity she could fit into her schedule. From consecutive honor rolls, Freshman Class President, the Student Government Association President, gospel choir member to Prom Queen, I'd say she had a great high school career.

When she left for college, Clarence III had us all to himself. He was the athletic one in the family who really enjoyed sports. We prayed through his academic challenges, but we were also witnessing a transformation that was spoken over his life when he was just 12 years old. A visiting minister prophesied that he would be a godly example to his peers. He also said he would be a millionaire in his teen years and seeded $100 into his future. Now, if you knew Mr. Rambunctious "BC" that is before Christ, you would have said "Humm," but we were witnessing this transformation before our eyes and waited with great expectation for what the Lord would do in his life. His passion for the Lord was so innocent and pure. It was beautiful to watch this young man growing up with such a zeal for the Lord and with godly standards. I often wondered if I loved the Lord as much as he did. I held those prophetic words close to my heart because they became the only anchor we had when things began to spiral out of control.

"Winding down from a long work week, two questions plagued my mind. 'God, what happened and how did we get here?' Facing the most heart-wrenching time of my life I felt powerless and void. I couldn't speak without tears. The pain cut so deep. But amid the perplexity of my mind, I was led to the Lord's Prayer, the first of many scriptures I learned as a child. And not until that moment did I have a real encounter with the prayer Jesus taught his disciples to pray. I now know without a doubt that God speaks in the midst of adversity and I'm more convinced than ever that He will never leave me. I began, *'Our Father which art in heaven. Hollowed be Thy name. Thy Kingdom Come. Thy will be done on earth as it is in heaven.'* Selah! With a long pause, the counsel of the Holy Spirit enlightened my thoughts, and my heart accepted the truth that God's promise on earth is a done deal in heaven. Thy will be done on earth is merely the place of the promise. I then understood 'As it is in heaven' is my 'And It Is So' on earth. I began to bless the Lord."

I wrote and read this excerpt for a theatrical role I played as a world-renowned author in October 2012. After the play and with a sense of urgency, a woman so moved by what she heard approached me and asked, "Where can I buy the book?" I explained that there was no book; but the conversation with God on Route 50 East was real, the unimaginable was real, and all the emotion we were trying to conceal was real. Clarence Jr. often reminds me that every house has a door and behind every door, there's a story. This just so happened to be our door and our painful story. It took some time for me to turn off the feelings of guilt, bewilderment, and despair. What happened to our son? We were watching him unravel and feeling completely hopeless. Things got worse long before they got better. It was spiritual warfare! Day by day sometimes minute by minute with only tears to articulate the hurt, I ran to God drawing strength from THE SOURCE greater than I; trusting Him who was indeed the only constant in our lives.

God's promises don't always come with explicit details. They often don't come with anything other than the promise while the process often remains a mystery taking you in unchartered directions as if you were moving forward by a force from behind. In an instance our home was turned upside down in such an intrusive way. While the master carpenter was carefully weaving and intertwining every delicate detail of our lives my heart felt like it had been ripped from my body. The depth of a mother's love is incomprehensible when she has to fight for the life of her child. How do you smile when the pain cuts so deep? Despite our continual prayers, there was a noise in the background screaming, "This is your new life!" The first emotion was fear on a mission to make this tragedy our new reality. We had no vantage point from which to draw that would make sense of what was happening or were we in denial.

We were enjoying the highs as proud parents of a soon to be college graduate in 2012. Yet, we struggled to understand what was happening to our son. He started his freshman year of college in North Carolina. He was a world traveler, so we had no reservations about him going away to school. And, while he had some concerns, we knew he could do it. The distress signals started early on. In his normal fashion he convinced us that he was ok and that he could finish out the year, but what we were experiencing continued when we brought him home. We determined then that he would not return to school for his sophomore year. We wanted to keep a close eye on him. He began detaching himself in a way that seemed like defiance at first, but his actions became more alarming as he continued to withdraw. We asked God, "What is this?" "How can this be?" "Lord, take it away." We spent many sleepless nights longing to see him well, as we watched him drift further and further away. We were void of answers. We blamed ourselves. Maybe we shouldn't have let him go so far away from home. Were we not listening to what wasn't being said? We asked ourselves, "Where did we go wrong?"

I wrote and performed a monologue entitled, "I Am the Hymn." Writing at the time was all I could do to articulate the pain in my heart. I tried to make sense of what was happening like that of slaves who wrote in code of their quest to be free. I wrote my own secret message from the titles of hymns searching for clarity in something I couldn't understand. In this portion of the monologue I spoke,

"The hymn caresses the back of God with songs of His sovereignty. Though my back be bent so low with tragedy that by all accounts would break the ordinary soul, in the midst of the loud noise of disappointment, the loud voice telling me its hopeless, give in to it and carry this burden like it's the promise, I yet hear a still small voice saying, "Peculiar woman, arise!" So, *Father, I Stretch My Hand to Thee. I Take my Burden to the Lord and Leave it There* for *I Will Trust in the Lord,* because *Great Is Thy Faithfulness.* I don't know about tomorrow, but *I Know Who Holds Tomorrow,* I know who holds my future, I know who holds my hand."

These hymns spoke to the depth of the longing in my soul. *"Great is Thy Faithfulness, Oh God My Father…"* I knew only God could heal the mind and change the heart. I cried longing to understand how something so horrible could happen to someone who loved God so passionately. I had to trust the God I was introduced to as a child; the same trust I had to now have for my own.

Songs of Deliverance

Singing in the church choir, at weddings, performing in productions throughout my high school and college years was pretty much how I spent my good spare time. I'd often hear from people in church even from my family how they could feel the presence of God through my singing. Trust me, it was by no action on my part, it was God's anointing on my voice. I could feel His presence as I nervously approached the mic. When I moved to Maryland and joined the Refreshing Spring Church of God in Christ that unexpected Sunday, Pastor Headen asked me where I wanted to serve and naturally I told him in the choir. I don't know if I ever loved singing because I always felt that weight of responsibility, but I understood my calling. The attacks started just a few months after I joined. It wasn't the pressure of moving to a new area or being a new bride. The enemy was cunning in his pursuit to muzzle my voice. He took some truth, added lies and whipped me into silence. He waited for the opportune time to attack. I became full of insecurity and fear almost paralyzing me on the inside and it showed up in my singing. It became a struggle to get out every note. I lacked the spiritual maturity to denounce the enemy's scheme to embrace the love and forgiveness that was already mine. I felt isolated in a room full of people, even sitting in the church. I was bound in a place I should have been free. I couldn't trust what was going on in my heart with anyone. Isn't that like the devil. His goal was to isolate me in an attempt to keep me from being free. But, I confided in the word of God and there is where I found solace. Psalm 32:1-7 spoke directly to me.

"Blessed is the whose transgression is forgiven, whose sin is covered. Blessed is the man unto whom the Lord imputeth not iniquity, and in whose spirit there is no guile. When I kept silence, my bones waxed old through my roaring all the day long. For day and night, thy hand was heavy upon me: my moisture is turned into the drought of summer. Selah. I acknowledge my sin unto thee, and mine iniquity have I not hid. I said, I will confess my transgressions unto the Lord; and thou forgavest the iniquity of my sin. Selah. For this shall every one that is godly pray unto thee in

a time when thou mayest be found: surely in the floods of great waters, they shall not come nigh unto him. Thou art my hiding place; thou shalt preserve me from trouble; thou shalt compass me about with songs of deliverance. Selah.”

I began writing song lyrics from the scriptures that seemed to hush the tormenting demons trying to conquer my soul. I continued to write and struggle and write and struggle and write, but I kept reading and running to the Lord. I wrote quite a few songs during those times. A few were sung by the children's ministry at church. I sent a compilation of songs to the United States Copyright Office under the title, “Surrounded by Songs of Deliverance.”

At the peak of our family crisis, the opportunity to record a couple of the songs couldn't have come at a better time. “They That Wait” would be my first recording. It was written some years ago for a health ministry program in honor of people who had overcome health challenges. How important that song would be personally just a few years later. I also wrote “Urgency” on September 11, 2001; the day the terrorists attacked our nation. I remember that day so clearly. Our nation was in a state of pandemonium as we tried to process the senseless act of hate. As I sat at work I began writing, “There's an urgency in my soul that makes me want to do more. There's an urgency in my soul telling me to press on. There's an urgency in my soul time is winding up so I must do what I must do for the Lord.”

The recording studio became the distraction I so desperately needed to escape from the realities of home, but the time to release the songs would have to wait. My vocals revealed every sign of sleep deprivation. There was no escape from the responsibility of home as we continued to try to process what was happening to our son. The weight of it was more than I wanted to bear. I struggled to remember the good times consumed by the pain wondering and asking God, “Why?” He didn't answer me right away, but He reminded me that I was still living a good life. In the midst of distress, He gave me one more song entitled, “Thank You for the Good Life.” I wrote, “It's not without struggle, not without strain, not without heartache, not without pain, but never forsaken You're always there to hear my cry to catch every tear. Thank You for the good life."

The only light I could see most days was the WORD coming out of my mouth as we watched the light fade from our son's eyes. I prayed that God would give him the mind of Christ. I would tell him he had the mind of Christ. You know real faith; that mustard seed faith, that loose knot of hope kind of faith wouldn't let me give up on my child. I had to believe that God was going to bring him out. I had to deny the voices clamoring for me to buy into hopelessness, even my own voice at times if I may be honest. I began to see God working in unexpected places showing us His unconditional love, giving us favor and giving me the assurance that He had a greater plan for our lives. What my natural eye was seeing would not be my son's fate. That kind of faith and determination made me a direct target of the enemy. His was now after me and little did I know that I would need even greater faith for myself.

The Silent Killer

Never in my wildest fear could I have imagined Thursday, May 29, 2014. Clarence Jr. was away on business, Avery was late coming home from work that evening, and Clarence III and I had just finished eating a delicious dinner, if I'd say so myself. After we finished, I began cleaning the kitchen and putting away the dishes. As I called Clarence III to come sweep the kitchen floor, I turned to him, and out of nowhere, I felt a sudden burning pain piercing me in the middle of my back. It felt like the hot tip of a javelin fiercely thrown tearing through my flesh. I paced the floor gasping for air struggling to inhale as I exhaled and spoke, "The blood of Jesus, the blood of Jesus" over and over again. I grew up calling on the name of Jesus, and I know without a shadow of a doubt that the blood of Jesus; drawing on the name of Jesus saved my life. There was nothing more. All I had and all I needed was His name.

I settled myself long enough to call my neighbor Kenda who lived just a few houses down the street. She didn't waste time coming. Still trying to breathe and I guess at the sight of me she asked if I wanted to go to the hospital. Within minutes the ambulance was at my door. We headed to Anne Arundel Medical Center in Annapolis, Maryland. On the way, it was all too strange when the emergency medical technician was notified that the hospital had no available beds. I was then taken to the Bowie Urgent Care Center not far from my home, and at that moment any medical facility was good enough for me. The nurse checked my blood pressure. The doctor on staff ordered an x-ray. He said he didn't want to expose me to too much radiation. I relied on his expertise to provide me with any explanation for the unusual pain. The x-ray returned revealed gas pockets and bowel in my intestine of which he determined to be constipation. Unprofessionally he said, "You're basically just full of _ _ _ _." I couldn't address his remark at that moment because the pain spoke louder than his ignorance. After several hours into the next morning, I was released from the urgent care center with instructions to take a fleet enema, drink plenty of fluids, take Milk of Magnesia and to follow up with my doctor if the pain persisted. Despite the outcome of the visit, there was a greater purpose for my release from that urgent care center that time would later reveal.

I didn't know the magnitude of what God was keeping me from all that day. By mid-afternoon after realizing that the pain was not going away, I called the Kaiser Permanente advice line. The nurse instructed me to go to the Kaiser South Baltimore Center in Baltimore, Maryland. When we arrived, I informed the physician on call of my earlier urgent care visit. I told him about the unusual burning pain. Upon sharing that information with him, he ordered a CT scan. As we waited, I saw the doctor abruptly leave the nurses station headed towards radiology. When he returned to my room in a very calm yet deliberate tone, he advised that I had an aortic dissection. I thought, "My aorta. Main artery. What is this?" I'd never heard of it before. He explained that there was a tear in my aorta. He said it was a type B dissection and didn't waste words in letting me know that my condition was critical. I still didn't fully understand what this was or what it meant for me. But, they were transporting me to the University of Maryland Medical Center (UMMC).

Avery left the Center to pick up Clarence Jr. from the airport. By the time they returned, the ambulance was transporting me to the UMMC shock trauma/critical care unit. Several nurses and physicians were awaiting my arrival ready to go to work. In minutes IVs were inserted for fluids, narcotics for the pain and aggressive blood pressure medications were administered to quickly lower my blood pressure. The doctors asked if I had experienced any trauma. I didn't have any trauma. Then they asked what I was doing at the time of the tear. I told them nothing out of the ordinary. I guess these questions were important to determine their next course of action. They confirmed that I had a Type B Dissection which meant that the tear in my aorta was descending from my heart down. A Type A Dissection is when the tear is ascending up into the heart. A tear in the aorta anywhere was dangerous. A Type B Dissection could potentially compromise or disrupt the blood flow to my major organs and lower extremities. If an aneurysm occurs or worse if it ruptures the outcome is generally fatal unless there is immediate medical attention or divine intervention. The tear itself threatened my life.

I received around the clock care. The nurses came to check my blood pressure, and to also check my pulse from my neck down to my feet. They were attentive to my every need. I remember a very kind nurse on the night shift so gently rubbed my back. Rubbing seemed to be the only relieve from the burning pain. She cared for me like I was her very own child. By divine order, I was in the best place because little did I know that the hospital's cardiac center specialized in aortic disease. God was working the miracle.

More Than a Notion, Just Enough Faith

By Sunday morning, my sisters Rosemary, Joanne and Pam, along with my nephews Chad and Chandler came from New Jersey to see me in the hospital. The look on my sisters' faces told my truth. They appeared to have had a better understanding of the severity of my condition than myself, but oh how much I needed to see my family. They asked questions and stayed for a while to make sure everyone was ok. Later that afternoon my soul sisters Patricia and Neci came to visit. I know they had already prayed for me. I also spoke with my Pastor James E. Jordan Jr. who I knew was praying for me along with my church family.

The doctors and residents did their rounds several times a day assessing my condition which wasn't a common occurrence. So, all of the staff was especially interested in my condition. At each visit, the reality of my situation became more and more clear. There was a sympathetic numbness in the doctor's delivery of my condition and the potential of death. One day I'm standing in my kitchen, and the next day I'm in shock trauma fighting for my life while still fighting for the life of another.

Now it's me. This person who always tried to care for everyone else is now in a state that only God can help. No one could help me. I laid in bed trying to process the threat of blood getting into the tear resulting in an aneurysm. I felt trapped in my own body hoping the excruciating pain away trying not to think the worst possibility. Dying from this condition could not be my end. Jesus help me!

What is this? How? Why? Why me? Where was my faith now? Was it in the same condition as my broken body? These were the questions running around in my mind. I was already in pieces emotionally struggling to understand how our lives took such a sharp turn, and now I'm fighting internal demons attempting to write the conclusion of my story. Two forces in fierce competition were in play, time as we waited for God to change our situation, and the enemy's cunning agenda baiting me away. His intent was to destroy me from the inside out. The stress of our family crisis gave way to emotions that almost had me leaving my home. I wanted to be free from the heavy burden I no longer wanted to carry. I wanted out. Period. That's what stress will do. But, now I'm physically torn lying flat on my back desperately needing God to save me from myself and my life. I came to the end of myself. I needed to come clean with God. He knows me; the real me. He knew all the thoughts running through my head. I needed Him more than I was willing to admit. Now I'm desperate for my life. I wanted to live, and I needed more than a miracle!

I bent the knees of my heart and pleaded for God's mercy and forgiveness. I knew I hadn't finished doing what He assigned me to do. I couldn't leave now. My husband needed me, my children needed me, and someone else was depending on me to pull through. This could not be my end. I prayed day and night fighting through the physical pain and tormenting death threats that came to override my faith. I couldn't articulate all of the emotion I was feeling, but God heard my heart's cry and His word became my defense. I began to truly believe and stand on the word of God. It's one thing to say it and another thing to act out what you say. *"I shall not die but live to declare the works of the Lord."* Psalm 118:17. *"He was wounded for our transgressions, bruised for our iniquity. The chastisement of our peace was upon Him, and with His stripes, we were healed."* Isaiah 53:5.

I was God's child, people! Jesus had already paid for my healing on the cross a long time ago. I began to declare God's word in my heart and out of my mouth. There are times you have to speak aloud what you believe. I reminded God of how He healed me of sciatica one Friday night during a youth revival service and then how He healed my knee in a Sunday morning service. My aorta by far out danced anything I'd ever gone through before, but I knew if God could heal me of those past conditions He had the power to heal me of this. I talked to my condition and told it that it had to line up with the word of God. The iron faith I had for everyone else I now had to have for myself. With this hit and a desperate need for healing I had to stretch beyond the common call for help. I waved a flag of surrender. I had to give it all to the Lord. This was my life!

After the shift change on Tuesday morning, a new nurse was assigned to my room. I will never forget Trisha. After she checked my vitals, she told me we were going for a walk around the unit before she washed me up. Wait! "Wash me up?" No stranger had ever washed me in my adult life! Now how was this going to work? I had to come to myself. After the last few days of sticky tape, gauze, wet wipes, and heavy medication, a wash up was necessary and to be honest I was too weak to completely help myself. Holding onto a stand-up walker, my legs nervously shaking like a newborn calf's and my breathing still compromised, I started walking. I couldn't help but notice as I passed other patients' rooms. They appeared unconscious, with their heads back, mouths open and tubes running everywhere. I must have forgotten where I was. You're in the ICU!!! Most patients in this unit can't do much at all. What was my problem? I'm moving ever so slowly trying to just breathe, but I'm talking, walking, mixing humor with pain, pushing my own call button, telling the nurses what I needed and how I was feeling, feeding myself what little I could eat and would eventually go to the bathroom by myself. Blessed me! God's mercy and grace!!!! Hallelujah! I cried with tears of grateful joy for my very life!

It's Real, Don't Give it a Pass

I began to tremble uncontrollably Tuesday evening. My skin was warm to the touch, but I was freezing on the inside. The nurse thought it might be due to the multiple medications, but the truth about this condition is that it's unpredictable. Each patient's experience is different. At Avery's request, the nurse secured a warming body bag which helped on one end, but I couldn't ignore another presence in the room. Hallucinations from the pain medications started soon after they were administered, but this feeling was unsettling and unlike anything I'd ever felt before. There was an unwelcomed visitor. I felt like my very life was being involuntarily snatched from my body. I couldn't put my finger on it until it became very clear to me. "An overwhelming sense of uncertainty and fear" is the definition for anxiety. I felt out of control of myself as I laid there simply helpless. Anxiety has a way of coming upon you unannounced. I struggled to keep my composure while anxiety tried to drive me out of my mind and my body. I know Clarence Jr. and Avery couldn't have known what was happening, but I know they were praying. I prayed within myself, "GOD HELP ME!" That spirit had to go. The next day my temperature and my blood pressure began to rise so the nurse had to remove the warming bag, and I had to remove the enemy again. There is power in prayer. I was weak in my body, but not out of my mind. *Submit to God, Resist the devil and he will flee from you.* James 4:7.

The Process

By day five, the medications administered by IV were replaced with oral medications. This was good news, but not without complications. Swallowing had become a problem. I also acquired a tract infection as a result of the catheter which meant one more oral medication. The nurses needed to also retain two IV lines; one just in case of an emergency and the other to draw blood. So, here we go again with more needles. The only problem was that my hands and arms were swollen, and bruise had become my new color. It was difficult for the nurses to access a vein to start the new IVs, so they had to use ultrasound. But, when they tried to access a vein, the vein would roll making it impossible to penetrate. A male nurse attempted to trap a vein ninja style by inserting two needles in a V formation. That proved to be painfully unsuccessful. After several attempts, they concluded that the next step would be to go through my neck. That was when I thought, "Now God!!!" Not soon after, a nurse they called "Super Nurse" came in, found a cluster of veins and secured one on the first attempt. Thank you, Jesus! Ask God first. Lesson learned!

I was moved to the step-down vascular unit late Thursday evening which meant that I was making great progress and the possibility of going home was near. Early Friday morning, Ms. Price was wheeled into the room to occupy Bed B. She and I would exchange pleasantries later that day. The doctors did their usual rounds at 6 a.m. They asked the same questions inquiring about my level of pain which was subsiding somewhat, but not good enough for me to go home.

Avery stayed with me that night and thank God she was there in the morning. As soon as the doctors left my room for whatever reason, I began throwing up. This was followed by an uncontrollable nose bleed resulting from a simple sneeze. These back to back episodes got the best of both of us. We began to cry out to God asking Him to stop the bleeding. Avery cried praying that God would just heal my body and allow me to go home. I wanted the same for myself more than she could imagine. I knew this ordeal had taken a toll on her, but she didn't leave my side. It wasn't long before the bleeding stopped and thank God because I needed to rest. My sister Rosemary arrived at the hospital that afternoon just in time to relieve Avery. Clarence Jr had been traveling from Bowie to Baltimore holding down our home while continuing to go back and forth to work. I was so glad Rosemary was there to relieve them.

Ms. Price and I got acquainted later that day. It was as if we'd known each other for years. We passed our short time together laughing and talking crazy pretending we had some great escape plan. The truth was we both needed around the clock care so complaining about not getting any rest from the constant interruptions was our problem to own and embrace. I enjoyed her humor as she talked over the dividing curtain comfortably interjecting in the conversations between my sister and me. I tell you old folks do what they want to do and say what they want to say. I took the same liberty of listening to her tell a male nurse who was preparing her for dialysis to watch what he was doing, or she was going to "whip" him! I hadn't heard that term in a while. Ms. Price was such a joy.

During this time, music was my escape from the noise. I listened to songs that brought a sense of peace and assurance. "My Destiny" by Kevin LeVar ministered to me throughout those dark days. "My destiny is too important to give up for anything." This one line lingered in my mind over and over again encouraging me to just hold on. "Keeper of the Door" by David and Nicole Bynum like so many others kept my mind on God's promises. The song said, "One thing I ask, and I will seek to drink the water from Your living well. My heart and flesh cry out Oh God, to know You in the place your glory dwells." The songs were so beautiful and soothing to my soul.

I woke up with a song on my heart the next morning. For whatever reason, I thought I could muster up enough breath to sing a little tune and I guess it was just enough for Ms. Price to hear. She said, "You can sing to me." I chuckled a bit because I was trying to exhale a tune, but I guess whatever she heard must have been music to her ears. I realized then that you never know how much just a little can be a blessing to someone else.

I was certain I was going home despite a little pain. By day nine, I was growing weary of the multiple needles, day after day along with each restless night. The doctors came to do their usual rounds, and after hearing that I would not be released that day, I got approval from my nurse to go and sit in the large lobby area around the corner from my room. The large windows from the fifth floor gave way to a view of the city of Baltimore, at least on the side I could see. I watched the workers and medical staff walking below from building to building crossing the major intersection going to and from their various destinations. I would have traded anything to be outside, but I sat at the window just taking it all in instantly revived by the sun. I made good friends with the staff, so they came looking for "Mrs. Jones" to take my meal order. I fell asleep, woke up, ate what I could of lunch and dinner right in the lobby. I also had two little visitors that day, my goddaughter, Lady Carrington and her brother Sir. Ronald III. It was such a joy to spend time with them. It later dawned on me that I didn't need one pain pill all day. The burning pain was gone.

Joy Comes in the Morning!

Thank God for Sunday morning! When the doctors came to do their rounds, I was happy to report no pain. With that news, I was released to go home but with very strict instructions. The heavy around the clock blood pressure medications would be a critical part of my daily regimen. This was required to keep my blood pressure and heart rate down. The doctors wanted to closely monitor the tear to see if an aneurysm might form. The most critical instruction was to seek immediate medical attention if I felt any sudden pain. I was scheduled for a repeat CT scan in August and an appointment was scheduled for me to meet with my primary care provider the next day, but guess what? I was going home. How great is our God!

I noticed Ms. Price hadn't received one visitor from Friday until Sunday morning which quickly changed when her family arrived in full force. They were celebrating a wedding that weekend which explained their absence. It was easy to see how much her family loved her. I'm sure that contributed to her warm demeanor. Before leaving, the Holy Spirit led me to ask if I could pray with her. My heart was racing with nervousness. Considering the number of people in the room, I wasn't sure how that was going to go. I obediently asked Ms. Price if I could pray for her, I bent over embracing her in my arms praying for her healing. She hugged me back and thanked me for the morning music. Wow! I tried to keep the volume at a respectable level, but I did want her to hear the songs that were blessing me. I knew they would be an encouragement to her as well. I had the craziest thought right at that moment. Did I go through all of this just for Mrs. Price? Surely, God could have let this happen another way, but even this was all in His plan.

I couldn't describe the joy I felt walking back into my home. No, I wasn't off and running which would have been my usual activity under more favorable circumstances. I wasn't doing much of anything at all. The intentionally debilitating medications kept me physically weak most of the time, but I was home and alive. I thought about the families whose loved ones never recover from this condition, to ever see them alive again. I knew God had extended His mercy to me. Belinda, my sister in love, Rosemary, Clarence Jr. and my children where there for me. God miraculously answered our prayer.

Clarence Jr and I met with my primary care provider the next day. Surprised, she greeted me with, "It's good to see you in the flesh!" To that I replied, "It's good to be seen in the flesh." She was shocked to learn that I had an aortic dissection. There was nothing in my history that would have suggested such a horrific event might occur. My last blood pressure screening before this time was lower than it had ever been. She couldn't explain it, but all I could do was thank the Lord for the outcome. She strongly expressed the importance of getting rest, taking the blood pressure medications as prescribed and to avoid lifting or carrying any heavy objects. She also suggested that I meet with a few of her colleagues for further instructions regarding my care. We left the office encouraged and hopeful that my aorta would heal.

I met with a nephrologist later that week who understood the impact this condition could have on my internal organs. Her area of expertise and concern was with my kidneys. She stressed that I take my medications as prescribed and to cut back or avoid any sodium intake if at all possible. While in the office she was able to show us the CT scan of my aorta and the line the tear formed from the top of my heart down. The shape of the view traveling down my aorta seemed to take on the form of a "J". My first thought was not Jaculin, but Jesus! He was all that came to my mind. If I could just think Him in this process, then I could believe Him for my healing.

Later that week I met with Dr. Nathaniel Dayes, the vascular surgeon who would be responsible for guiding my care going forward. He reviewed the scan and was very candid about my reality and the complexities of this condition. He shared that surgery would be inevitable. He delivered the same message for me to rest and to make sure I took my blood pressure medications as prescribed. In my follow up visit, he recommended that I meet with one of his colleagues who specialized in aortic disease. He trusted his expertise to further assess my care.

My goddaughter Adrienne and her mom Michele came to visit not shortly after I returned home. They were concerned as others were wanting to know what happened. As I tried to explain, I became short of breath. It felt like the onset of the initial tear as the pain and breathlessness began to overwhelm me. I couldn't talk anymore. I called Clarence Jr. to let him know what was happening, so he headed right home. I felt like I was leaving this earth, but *"Better is a neighbor who is near than a brother far away"* Proverbs 27:10. I called my neighbor Patricia, who God purposely placed right next door. This woman of God was a sister unfailing. When I called, she and Pastor Robert Johnson came to my home. She gently rubbed the anointing oil on my legs as they prayed calling on the name of the Lord for my healing. The death threats had to give way to the power in Jesus' name. My breathing returned to normal, and the burning pain in my back began to subside. The feeling of hopelessness had to leave in the name of Jesus!

I couldn't account for any deed done on my part to warrant the outpouring of love from my family, neighbors, church family, friends and even strangers who learned of my condition. My sisters Chaneta and Joanne came from New Jersey to spend time with me. My neighbors and church family checked on me regularly, calling and preparing meals for me and my family. I thanked God for my village. There's no impassioned word to describe the love that was shown to us during that time. Every meal, call, text message, drive by and cards too numerous to count were so appreciated, but the prayers of the righteous availed much. Beyond my immediate circle of family and friends, people were literally praying for me around the world. They were believing God for me to pull through. I was holding on.

Happy Anniversary to Us

It's our anniversary June 25th twenty-six years to the day. Yes, I could imagine being married that long and the last two years were the most challenging of all. We knew this condition along with what we were already going through had changed our lives forever. But, on this day, I recognized the privilege of being married to such a man God gave to me. This man took the vows for better for worse, in sickness and health to his heart. He fought for the life of what he calls "My family." The strength of our love had been tested, but the mercy of God kept us strong. My circumstance was not going to change that, nor the way we would celebrate special occasions. Clarence Jr. was insistent that we go away this year to celebrate our anniversary. I had my reservations about traveling any distance from home especially with concern that a medical facility might not be close enough if I should need it, but I had to honor my husband. More importantly, I had to trust God to take care of us no matter where we might go.

We headed south. I slept most of the way, but it didn't seem long before we arrived at our destination. I looked out the window and watched Clarence Jr. go to check us into the hotel negotiating every step I would need to take to get to the entrance. I knew it was going to take every breath. As I walked in, the carpet pattern in the hotel foyer and hallway to our room intensified the dizziness and labored breathing I was already experiencing. I remember walking, telling myself to just keep looking up. That was a revelation in and of itself. Keep looking up made all the difference in the world that day. Thank God, our room was right in the middle of the hallway. I made it!

We rested for a little while and then headed to my favorite place. My husband knew exactly what would lift my spirit. As we searched for a park, all I could see in front of me was blue. God had a parking space with my name on it just a few feet away from the water. Carrying only myself, I walked across the sand, took a seat underneath the beach umbrella, wrapped myself in a blanket, and with the warmth of the summer breeze sweeping over my cold body nothing was more beautiful than the view in front of me.

Despite my labored breathing, cold, and still physically weak body we returned to the water the next day. As we slowly walked along the boardwalk, I couldn't help but notice a mother duck walking across the sand with all seven of her ducklings, as the waves rolled in and out ever so close to their feet. I watched how she instinctively guided them to the water's edge which could have carried her babies away in an instance, but it was as if she knew just how close to let them walk. They were familiar with the water I imagined, but not the force of the rippling waves. I thought about God who never said we wouldn't have trouble. In fact, He said we would have trouble even as Jesus faced trouble. Jesus had to go to the cross, but in John 16: 32-33 he leaves the disciples with these words. *"Behold, the hour cometh, yea, is now come, that ye shall be scattered, every man to his own, and shall leave me alone: and yet I am not alone, because the Father is with me. These things I have spoken unto you, that in me ye might have peace. In the world ye shall have tribulation: but be of good cheer; I have overcome the world."* It was by no coincidence that God would allow me to capture this visual. Trouble might come, and for me trouble had come, but He was not going to leave me. He was going to lead me. He was going to deliver me.

Hold On

I tried so hard to hide all of the emotion I was feeling to be strong for my family, but I couldn't hold back the tears this particular day. The weight of my son's condition coupled with my own physical ailment and pain fell on me like a ton of bricks. I remember holding my head to a vent just to breathe feeling without strength even for myself. But, God sent my son to rescue me that day. Clarence III walked into my room anxiously wanting me to see a video clip of Tye Tribett singing or should I say praising to, "He Turned It!" In his normal old goofy way which always made me laugh he said, "Come on mom, let's dance!" With the little strength I had, he took me by my hands, pulled me to my feet and we started to dance. Trust me, it was the shortest dance ever, but it was a declaration that God was going to turn things around for both of us. Our "IT" had to go! Everyone has one, and I was believing God for our situation to turnaround. The devil thought he had us. He thought our lives were over. He thought that we would give up. He thought that we had no more, but that's when someone greater stepped in our situation. Our new morning had to begin because like in the lyrics of the song, I was believing God to change our situation.

I knew my strength would be revived if I could just get to the church house. I slowly dressed myself Sunday after Sunday. Yes, I even put on my high heels. They were of course sitting shoes. My family was quite protective, but they took me to church as often as I was able. My church was full of huggers which was not good for me at the time due to the burning pain in my back. With the wisdom from my Pastor, I came to church late and left early. But, every time I entered the church doors God did not disappoint. He was in the house! It was better than the Super Bowl half time show or the NBA finals. The praises went up, and the blessings came down. Pastor Jordan encouraged the congregation to just praise the Lord. His messages encouraged me to praise the Lord with the confidence that God was going to bring me out. We praised the Lord until hope started screaming "LIVE!!!" Every week I found myself getting better and better.

I asked my primary care physician if we could adjust the blood pressure medications to help me regain my strength. She was pleased with my progress and agreed to lower the dosage just enough. I continued to progress and not long after, I was given the all clear to return to work. I understood my return would be with restrictions, but I so desperately needed to regain a sense of normal. I adhered to her instructions, situations were slowly improving at home, my repeat CT scan was scheduled for August 12th and I was released to go back to work the next day.

My co-workers greeted me with warm welcomes especially from those who understood the severity of my condition. I was a miracle walking in the flesh! Of course, I had to get acclimated in my new role, but I was glad to get back to work. Wednesday was a great day. Thursday was even better. By Friday I thought I was on my way to full recovery. Clarence Jr. and I carpooled those few days and had plans to meet friends for dinner later that Friday evening. I was a little tired but looked forward to going out. As we drove home, I started feeling a little discomfort in my chest. The feeling wasn't completely unfamiliar, but as the night progressed the pain became more intense, and I became more concerned. I snuck away to take communion which was important to me and yes, I prayed. In the early morning hour, I called the Kaiser health advice line. After sharing a few blood pressure readings, I was instructed to go to the St. Agnes Hospital emergency room in Baltimore, Maryland.

I wasn't immediately taken to the treatment area by the intake representative until the nurse read my intake form and realized the severity of my condition. She started moving with a sense of urgency as did everyone in the emergency room. The ER physician shared that the hospital didn't have anyone on staff trained in "Aortic Disease" so I would be transferred to another hospital. My insurance ordered that I be taken to the Washington Hospital Center in Washington, D.C., but the physician advocated that I be transported back to the UMMC which was our preference. I listened to her pleading my case as her voice elevated almost frustrated with the person on the other end of the phone. Then entered the unwelcomed visitor making another appearance with a loud silent presence this time. It started at my feet. I felt it creeping up my legs.

ANXIETY is real! It manifests itself just at the time when you're the most vulnerable. I wanted to jump out of bed; and run around the hospital. My husband stood strong assuring me I was ok. And with the same intensity to fear, I had to trust God, resist the devil, and he had to flee.

I was welcomed with open arms by some of the same nurses who cared for me during my initial admission. After four days of intense treatment to lower my blood pressure, I was released from the UMMC. I advocated for my release because I had an appointment scheduled with Dr. Robert Crawford, the colleague Dr. Dayes recommended that I should see. He had already reviewed the recent CT scan and compared it to the initial scan taken in May. He was very tactful in sharing that my aorta had grown twice the expected size from the time of the initial tear. He said it had become "aneurystic" and surgery was more than a suggested next step. It was unavoidable. My case had already been brought before the board of physicians who unanimously agreed that I was a good candidate for the cutting-edge procedure to repair my aorta. He said he would give us time to think about my decision, but to not think too long.

I was believing God for a miraculous healing. Yes, the way He healed me in the past I thought surely, He could heal me without surgery. Thank God for the wisdom of my good sister-friend Pam. She was a woman of faith who I'd grown to love and respect. Our professional relationship turned into an unbreakable sisterhood and one that meant complete honesty. When I shared with her that I was believing God for my healing and didn't want to have surgery, she didn't waste words in reminding me that not everyone is a candidate for the procedure and perhaps this was the way God wanted to heal me. I remembered that it was by no coincidence the unforeseen path resulting in my admission to the UMMC in the first place and later learning that this hospital had a well-known aortic disease clinic. In addition, Dr. Dayes understood the complexity of my condition and the necessary post-operative care I would need following surgery. He recommended and advocated that the procedure be done at this hospital; and Dr. Crawford was skilled to do the procedure. God was already in the details. I just needed to trust Him. If I was going to go through it, I was going through it with God.

Patience

I remember one night waking up out of my sleep in a panic. I was fighting to breathe. It was as if someone was holding my nose with their hand over my mouth. I gasped for air asking myself, "What is this?" The death threats were real, and this devil was out to kill me. But, I found rest again in God's word. As I read I came across Psalm 3:5. *"I lay down and slept, I awaked, for the Lord sustained me."* The Lord was my Sustainer. My time was in His hands. Though, the enemy was relentless in his pursuit, he was no match for the word of God. He came, but he could not prosper. We have to remember the power of God's word and use it. This was another lesson.

The time of waiting often reveals a lot about one's self, our true character. If I was honest with myself, I lacked real patience. Waiting on God to change our family situation and now needing God to heal me required patience. I needed help with my basic needs which was new for someone used to doing things for herself. Patience kept ringing in my ear. I thought about James 1:3 that says, *"My brethren, count it all joy when you fall into various trials, knowing that the testing of your faith produces patience."* I asked myself how in the world can I count what I was going through as joy. My flesh was speaking. I wondered within myself when all of this would be over. If I may be honest, it felt like it was never going to end. We don't like to admit it, but sometimes in our walk, we get weary especially when an illness strikes or when we encounter something that feels too heavy to endure. I began searching this scripture in James and came across C.H. Spurgeon's sermon commentary preached on February 4, 1883. I abruptly stopped in my tracks when I read this paragraph.

"It is by our faith we are saved, justified and brought near to God and therefore it is no marvel that it is attacked. It is by believing in Christ that we are delivered from the reigning power of sin and receive power to become the sons of God. Faith is as vital to salvation as the heart is vital to the body: hence the javelins of the enemy are mainly aimed at this essential grace. Faith is the standard bearer, and the object of the enemy is to strike him down that the battle may be gained. If the foundations be removed what can the righteous do? If the cable can be snapped whither will the vessel drift? All the powers of darkness which are opposed to right and truth are sure to fight against our faith, and manifold temptations will march in their legions against our confidence in God."

The same way I described the pain from the tear was the same way Spurgeon described the attack against our faith. The enemy's attempt was to make me lose faith in God's ability to heal my son and to also poke holes at my faith for my own healing, but he had to succumb to the truth of God's word. I had to continue to believe by faith. Faith tested develops patience, endurance, and strength. I got it! The trying of my faith was working patience. Yes, faith grows through trials, tribulations and even torn aortic experiences.

I was further astounded when I came across Psalm 11:3, *"If the foundations be destroyed, what can the righteous do?"* My mom, a short little feisty woman of God who spoke the Word with authority and power, quoted this scripture in her strongest voice on her home voicemail. I thought, "What in the world?" Whenever I heard her message, I would think she could have left a little kinder message. It went like this, "If the foundation be destroyed, what can the righteous do? Please leave a message." I remember respectfully exchanging words with her about this, but she wasn't as she would say, "studdin" me. What she did say was that one day I would understand. Her communication had declined during her illness, and she was bedridden just before her death, but she had full clarity when she talked about the Lord. We spent time reading the Bible which was soothing to her soul. I'll never forget the day as I read to her and came across this verse. It all became clear, and I then understood the reason for the passion in her voicemail message. Our hope is in the Lord even if the bottom falls out. God is our foundation. God was faithfully holding mommy up with His strong right hand. As I sat at her bedside that evening, tears of joy rolled down my face just amazed at her faith in God.

I Remember Mama

The day I witnessed mommy leave this life headed for eternity will forever be engrained in my heart. The day before I told her, "Tomorrow it's just going to be you and me." I'd been traveling from Maryland to New Jersey almost every weekend to care for her along with my sisters. We'd done all we knew to do. My sisters were acting doctors and nurses. We enjoyed some of our best times and best laughs over the few months after removing her from the nursing facility. We were a force to be reckoned with as we took care of her at home. No one could have done it the way we did. Her communication had declined, but she would periodically break out and say, "Hush! Hush! Just listen. You don't know nothin'!" My sisters and I thought ok, but as we look back on those days we find ourselves apologizing to her even today. We've grown to understand that mommy was right. We really don't know anything. Life continues to teach us that we don't know what we don't know. We have to listen.

Her transition from this life to glory was on December 11, 2007. I'll never forget the night before she passed. I panicked when she stopped breathing, but my sister Joanne said she had been doing that a lot, which was not comforting for me. I thought it was going to be over then, but she kept my word when I told her tomorrow it was just going to be her and me. I left the house that Monday morning to place an employment acceptance letter in the mail. I was consulting with a healthcare company a few months prior and decided to accept a permanent full-time opportunity.

When I returned to the house that afternoon the hospice nurse, who just so happened to be a friend of the family, was leaving. As Rosemary walked her out of the house, I stood at the foot of mommy's bed. I saw a look on her face that I had never seen before. Her eyes were fixed as she looked over my shoulder with a longing that seemed to satisfy. It was if she was reaching forward as I watched her take in and release her last breath. That moment was indescribable! It was beautiful! She was free from every ache, pain, headache, heartache, denial, and disappointment. The struggle was over. She was with the Lord; no turning back. The look on her face said it all. Oh, that I may really know Him! That is what I long for; an inward longing to really know Him. Intimacy with Him is my continual desire and the promise to be with Him in due time.

Another Attack

Moving about, weak, but determined. I continued to encourage myself in the Lord and was thankful for the support of my family and friends. I continued to work and attended church which was the highlight of my week. Clarence Jr. and I tried our best to maintain some sense of normal at home which was challenging at times, but we were managing. We had the opportunity to attend the 10th Church Anniversary of God Glorified Church of God in Christ. Pastor Joseph Gray was my former Assistant Pastor. He had also been instrumental in my spiritual walk, so I wouldn't have missed this event for the world. I was excited to see other church members who I hadn't seen for a long time. Those who knew of my condition had been praying for me, so it was a blessing to share in this occasion with them. The evening was even more special when Kevin Levar sang "My Destiny." That song ministered to me as I laid in shock trauma wondering about my life. To hear it live fortified my resolve that I was going to make it. Oh, how God will put you in places that remind you of His goodness and your destiny!

We left the celebration and headed home. It wasn't before long after dozing off to sleep in the car I remember waking up throwing my head forward. For whatever reason I couldn't swallow my own natural spit. You know how you just swallow? No thought, you just do it. I had to intentionally force myself to swallow. This sensation continued throughout the next day, and by that evening I was back in the hospital. Dr. Crawford wanted to determine if the aneurysm might have grown, possibly pushing against my esophagus. I told myself, "Not so." I had to let the devil know, not today. Thank God there was no swelling and no change in the CT scan which was always good news. The doctor concluded that perhaps this sensation was due to the combination of medications I was taking. Whatever the cause I was learning to lean on God. *"Be anxious about nothing, but in everything, by prayer and supplication with thanksgiving, let your requests be made known to God. And the peace of God, which surpasses all understanding, will guard your hearts and your minds in Christ Jesus,"* Philippians 4:6-7. I was released with instructions to just rest until surgery.

The Big Day

Friday, October 31st at 7:30 a.m. was game time. I arrived at the UMMC with my family. They had been with me every step of the way. After being prepped for surgery, Dr. Crawford came to my room to explain the details of the surgery. He said they would first need to re-route a smaller artery coming off my aorta supplying blood to my left arm to the carotid artery. I'm no physician, so I had to go with it. He would then proceed with coiling the area of the tear and then graft and stent the main section of my aorta. He also told me that a lumbar drain would be placed in my back to monitor any fluid build-up on my spine during the surgery. He was very candid in sharing the possibility of paralysis which was one of the risks of the procedure. This procedure could affect my ability to walk. He also informed us that the procedure would be done laparoscopically unless there was a complication resulting in an open chest procedure. I didn't have an ear to entertain any of the risks at this point. I was in a state of complete dependence on God. The lead anesthesiologist also came to inform me of his role during the surgery. He introduced me to two residents who would be observing the procedure as well. After praying with my family, I entered the operating room at 12:12 p.m.

The first order of business once the supporting cast entered the operating room was to ask everyone to let me see their hands. Then I asked if they would hold them up. Looking puzzled and a bit hesitant, they raised their hands. Then I said, "God, You got this!" I sat on the side of the operating table as the lead anesthesiologist attempted to insert the needle in my back for the epidural. After two failed attempts, the one male resident seeing my visible pain, gently put his hand on my shoulder. There was something in his touch that assured me that I was going to be ok. He told me to just relax and to those words, I blacked completely out. When I came to myself, the lead anesthesiologist was apologetically laying me down on the operating table. The procedure hadn't begun. For just a split second I thought, "Now what is this?" Then I was out for the count. It didn't seem like five hours had passed before

Clarence Jr. and Avery were standing over me smiling with faces of relief. Praise the Lord, oh most high!! It was undeniable! Indisputable! God did it!

Despite the burning in my chest and having to lay flat on my back, I was alive! One can only understand the enormity of that feeling if their life has ever hung in the balance. A lot happens during surgery and you generally don't know to what extent, if at all. After surgery, I felt an antenna-like tube sticking out my neck, the drain remained in my back and I felt dried blood stuck to my scalp. But, none of that could compete with being present in the world. I knew to be absent from the body is to be present with the Lord, but it wasn't my time. God was good to me!!!

I asked to have the bars on my bed lowered so I could stretch my arms. It would be a couple of days before the drain would be removed so I had to lay straight. I would pay for that request the next day as my chest burned from all the internal work that had been done and the over stretching. But, when I touched my chest there were no scars. Thank you, Jesus. The doctors and interns still fascinated by the procedure came to do their rounds several times a day. Some came to visit out of routine. I had to turn one resident away. Pray for me! The nurses and interns received on the job training on how to drain the fluid from my spine. I listened and watched intently as the doctors gave careful instructions on how much fluid to drain and when to drain it. Any misstep could have compromised my ability to walk.

I wasn't sure if the visit from the lead anesthesiologist was standard post-operative protocol. He apologetically shared that two anesthesiologists were called to assist with inserting the drain in my back. I could see the concern on his face, but God had His hand on me. When the drain was removed, I was able to sit up, get up, get out of bed, stand up and walk! My legs were weak, but I was walking! Some might say walking was what should have happened, but I was thanking God for what didn't happen. God was showing Himself strong!

I was assigned a male nurse named Messi that Tuesday morning. I believe that was the spelling. Mess-i? Yes, Messi! Too close. He was very attentive carefully helping me in and out of bed. I spent most of Wednesday sitting up thanking God for the miracle. That afternoon I fell asleep in my chair and was sleeping pretty well until I was scared awake. Messi rushed into my room to take me to radiology. I wasn't fully awake and by then very nervous. The thought of going to radiology was unsettling. Radiology had not been kind to me in the past. The hospital transporter came to take me, but Messi was adamant that he would take me. My body shook all the way there, but he reassured me over and over again that everything was going to be alright. He stayed in the room while the technician prepared my IV and when the scan was complete it seemed within seconds Messi was standing over me saying, "See, I told you I wouldn't leave you." He wheeled me back to my room, and thank God not long after I arrived, I was given the good report. The surgery was a success. Hallelujah! I was moved to the step-down vascular unit later that night. I was one step closer to going home.

I settled into the step-down unit. My vital signs were checked by my new nurse. After he finished, I remember asking him his name, and when he said "Noel", there lied another Selah. Messi and Noel? My mind immediately reflected back to the very beginning and it all became clear. It was in God's plan for me to be taken to the Bowie Urgent Care Center rather than Anne Arundel Medical Center. From there I would have been transferred to Washington Hospital Center. Kaiser's South Baltimore Center transported me to the UMMC. The UMMC was not a contracted facility with my insurance, but the aortic disease clinic was there. Dr. Dayes advocated for my surgery to be done at the UMMC where the expertise and post-operative care I would need was best. And after the four hospital admissions, my last two nurses' names were Messi and Noel. Jesus was with me all the time. I couldn't have scripted the course of these events for myself. God did it just for me and for His glory! I got to tell it!

Good Friday

I felt like life had been poured back into me. I knew it was a miracle. Even going through the process was miraculous. I was alive to see another day. I was discharged on Friday and was glad to be home. But, by Sunday my right side felt like it was going to explode. I couldn't explain it or ignore it. I dared not utter a single word to my family. They had already been through enough. The Lord led me to think about what was different this time. I recalled a visit from Dr. Jackson, the Hypertensive Specialist while in the hospital. He explained that I was automatically thrown into the vascular disease category due to the aortic dissection. He said I would need to add a cholesterol medication to my regimen going forward. I was given Pravastatin the day of discharge and continued to take it until Sunday. I began researching the side effects of Pravastatin, the blood pressure medications, pain medication and Tylenol all of which could potentially have an impact on my liver. My liver, of course, was on my right side. I was familiar with the blood pressure medication, pain medication and Tylenol. So, by a process of elimination, the Pravastatin had to be the culprit. But, with the exception of the blood pressure medications, I stopped taking everything. I researched natural alternatives that might help cleanse my liver. When I learned that lemons and green leafy vegetables would help, I began eating them in abundance.

We met with Dr. Crawford for my post-operative follow up appointment later that week. He seemed to be more excited to see us than we were to see him. He was so proud of the outcome of the surgery. He shared the before and after video of how my aorta was functioning as a result of the tear. Prior to the surgery, my blood was traveling down my aorta but was slowing, trickling up into the tear resulting in the aneurysm. The surgery was a success and it was a miracle without a doubt. I shared with him the pain in my side and the preventive measures I took to help myself. Perhaps the tone in my voice suggested that I may have been doing too much reading. He recommended, however, that I have my aorta rescanned in three months rather than six months and suggested that I keep my appointment with Dr. Jackson.

We met with Dr. Jackson later that day. I advised him of the unusual pain and inquired about more natural alternatives to take rather than the Pravastatin. He recommended a different statin which was not a reasonable option considering the pain. He asked if I had a liver function test while I was in the hospital. With access to my hospital records, he was able to check if one had been completed. He immediately left the room and returned instructing me to stop taking the Pravastatin and to have another liver function test done right away. The test in the hospital revealed that my liver count was very high to be prescribed a statin at all, at least not at that time. God knows everything. He led me to discontinue the medication and to research foods that would help cleanse my liver naturally. I took the liver function test the following week, and by then my numbers had returned to normal levels. Through seen and unseen danger, I had already come. We serve a great God!

I was healed, but the process of healing was long. There were days I wanted to remove all that was physically holding me together. No one really talks about the recovery process and the impact it has on the person. It is often more challenging than the ordeal itself. Those were the days the subtle thoughts of dying would come to disrupt my peace, but I had to cancel every thought. I spent time tuning into Christian programming that ministered life, faith, and hope. I was watching Creflo Dollar one particularly difficult day. He was holding up his hands declaring, "Jesus has the keys of death, hell, and the grave. The enemy can't take my life. God is in control of my day of departure." Those words continued to help build my faith. God told me to choose life, and I shall live to declare His mighty works. It didn't matter how I felt, this was His promise. I shall live!

I Got Another Testimony

I wasn't sure if I was physically ready to return to work, but I had to keep moving on. I know some of my co-workers were not expecting me to return and if the enemy had his way, he would have made sure of it. But, GOD knew I would tell of His goodness! Not only was I blessed to come back, but even my pay had to return to my account. My new position started the Monday after the aortic dissection occurred. The first blessing was that I was paid short term disability off of my new salary. During my recovery from surgery; however, I was informed that my disability benefits had been exhausted and that I would not be paid again until after I returned to work. When I returned to work in December, I was instructed to contact the short-term disability office. During my conversation with the representative, she informed me that I should have been paid for the month of November. Well, I didn't ask one question. The very next pay period I was paid for all of November along with my new regular pay.

God's principle of reaping and sowing start with our obedience. Malachi 3:10 says, *"Bring all the tithes into the storehouse that there may be food in My house. And try Me now in this, says the LORD of hosts, If I will not open for you the windows of heaven and pour out for you such a blessing that there will not be room enough to receive it."* I honored God with the tithe and offering, and He in turn was faithful to me.

The repeat CT scan was scheduled for February 9th. My family didn't go with me for the scan, but everybody came to the follow up appointment to hear the results. We were all relieved to receive the good report. Dr. Dayes advised that there was no change which meant that my aorta had not grown, and the surgery was successful. I must admit I was a little anxious, but we could only thank God for what He had done. Dr. Dayes was very candid in telling me that if I wanted to live, I would have to take blood pressure medications for the rest of my life. I would also need to be rescanned annually. I trusted that even the blood pressure medications would not be needed one day. Dr. Dayes recommended that I follow up with Dr. Crawford regarding one additional question I had regarding the scan.

I sent Dr. Crawford a text February 25, 2015.

Me: "Hi Dr. Crawford. Hope all is well. I met with Dr. Dayes last week and your office has received my scan. From what he shared they look pretty good. I'm hoping you will say the same. I understand there is still a slight opening, but we anticipate it will close completely. Please let me know if I need to see you. I only want to see you to say thank you. I'm starting to feel like my better self. I'll check with your assistant over the next few weeks to see when you will be in. Have a great day."

Dr. Crawford: "I just looked at it. It looked good. The small blush is called a Type 2 Endo Leak. Nothing to do. Repeat scan in 6 months. Entire Aorta."

Me: "Thank you so much. The Lord has gifted your hands. Ok. Will do."

I began experiencing nerve pain after the surgery. Without warning, the pain would start in my lower back and permeate down my legs. It would occur more frequently while lying in bed but would also start almost anywhere at any time. God had already healed me of sciatica, so I was familiar with this pain. I could only attribute it to the multiple attempts to insert the epidural in my back prior to the surgery. I met with a neurologist who recommended surgery as a last resort if it worsened, but another surgery was not an option. The Lord told me to start moving before the pain had an opportunity to travel. Guess what? No medication. No surgery. No more pain. Just moving faith in God.

Thank You Pastor Jordan

Pastor Jordan sent a picture taken of me some time prior to the aortic dissection. Only God could have known how much I needed the encouragement the day I received it. The visual was a prophetic word letting me know that I wasn't finished singing, lifting my hands and giving God the glory. I didn't return to directing the choir but making a joyful noise unto the Lord was in order. The perfect time for a come-back was Pastor's Anniversary September 2015. We praised the Lord that Sunday. What an honor it is to have a leader who as he says, "Smells like sheep." He serves to meet the needs of the congregation God has placed in his care. This picture spoke life to me. Thank you, Pastor Jordan for every prayer, call and picture. Thank you for listening to that still small voice!

A New Year, Another Test

Christmas 2015 was met with another unexpected event. We spent the days in between Christmas and the New Year nursing Clarence III's right eye almost shut closed from the shingles. Clarence Jr. and Avery worked in the communications ministry at church, so they attended the New Year's Eve watch night service while we stayed home. It was a rare occasion for the family to be separated on that night, but that was our reality. I watched the evening news highlighting the main events of the year, wondering what life would bring us in the new year. In our normal fashion, we rang in the New Year on our knees thanking God for allowing us to see another year.

We waited for a call or text message from Clarence Jr. or Avery shouting, "Happy New Year!" When Avery sent a video clip of the service, everything at that moment took a back seat to what we were witnessing. Pastor Josh Wilson was walking across the front of the church! Our friend had been stricken with sickness for over a year, laid flat on his back most of that time, coded several times, and now he's walking across the front of the church in the flesh! Immediately, as if it was a new revelation, I thought if God could work a miracle for him as He had already done for me, I knew the promise of healing my son completely was on the way. Immediately, I finished wiping the tears from my eyes. Clarence III then asked me to anoint his eye. I did, and it was so. The swelling in his eye began to go down.

I sang in the choir First Sunday, January 2016. It was a joyous service, but if I may be so honest, I couldn't help thinking about what the year might bring for us. As I praised the Lord, it came to me ever so strong that anything I wanted that year, I was not only going to have to fight for it, but I was also going to have to fight to keep it. Little did I know how true this would be. But, the one difference I had this time was big history with God.

Shortly after the aortic dissection, I began hearing an unsettling ringing in my ear. I couldn't shake it. I followed up with my primary care physician who suggested that I meet with the vascular surgeon. I met with Dr. Dayes who confirmed that it was not vascular related, but I couldn't dismiss the ringing. I knew this irritant was not a figment of my imagination. I followed up with my primary care physician again. She thought I was anxious, given my past medical history and recommended that I meet with a therapist, or perhaps take a little pill to help manage any feelings of anxiety. The other recommendation was that I follow up with an ear, nose, and throat (ENT) doctor. That seemed to be the most logical next step.

I called the Kaiser appointment line to schedule an appointment with the ENT, and while on the phone, the representative reminded me that it was time for my routine mammogram screening. I thought the following Monday was as good a day as any. That Tuesday following the exam, I received a call advising that I needed to return for a repeat mammogram. It wasn't the first time I needed a repeat mammogram, so I had no worries. I was also too busy with work to concern myself. I returned for the exam on February 26th. I had the mammogram, an ultrasound and a breast biopsy on that very same day. The following Monday, I received "The Call". The radiologist who performed the biopsy informed me that cancer was found in my right breast; Ductal Carcinoma. I felt a three-second sting in the pit of my stomach as I guess one might have felt hearing such shocking news. I quickly responded as if I was responding to an inquiry at work with, "What next?" The radiologist explained that the cancer was confined to the duct, it was in the very early stages, so she was confident that it was treatable, and that everything would be fine. She told me to expect a call the next day from a nurse who would schedule my next appointment with a team of physicians. She asked if I was ok and to that my reply was yes. I mean, what was cancer to me anyway? I called Clarence Jr. who calmly took the news and suggested that we wait to tell the children until after my appointments.

I was in the middle of a 26-week certification program at the Refreshing Spring Church of God in Christ Bible Institute. Despite the news, I went to class that Tuesday evening.

Missionary Marshburn was the instructor for the Communion and Water Baptism course. She passionately taught on the significance of the Lord's table calling it "The table of healing." This was not by coincidence. I began applying the cancer diagnosis to the table. Jesus sacrificed his life on the cross and paid the price in His body not only for us to have fellowship with Him, but He nailed all sicknesses and disease to the cross. I didn't share the cancer diagnosis with the class, but I was overjoyed as the instructor went into depth about the significance of the communion table. God's forgiveness of my sins through Jesus' sacrifice on the cross was my assurance of access to the table of healing. Lord, It's me again!

We met with a team of doctors Thursday of that week. My first visit was with Dr. Samana Zulu, the general surgeon. He explained that I had Triple Negative Breast Cancer, which meant that the three most common receptors to fight this aggressive form of cancer were not present in the tumor in my breast. Chemotherapy and radiation by industry standards were the recommended treatments to decrease the possibility of a reoccurrence. Dr. Cooper, the oncologist, explained the chemotherapy process and the possible duration of the treatment. Dr. Patel, the radiation oncologist, shared the steps following chemotherapy. Radiation would be directly targeted at the area where the cancer was found. My last appointment that day was with a genetic counselor who suggested that I take the BRAC test which is a blood test taken to determine if I had the genetic gene for breast cancer. This would have been especially important for my daughter. Thank God, no gene.

I reflected on the day trying to process what I didn't fully understand. It had only been fifteen months since the aortic dissection repair. My body was still adjusting to that trauma and now cancer. The word cancer took on a whole new meaning, because it was now me. I didn't blame God, but I asked why. Why this? Why me? Is my body just breaking down or was there something more?

Stand

Avery was relentless in her pursuit for her slightly overweight parents to get in shape. She had the fortunate opportunity to meet a personal trainer who offered in home services. She invited him to our home just a few weeks prior to the cancer diagnosis, and how important exercise would be for my overall health. After the first trial workout with MAC Fitness, LLC, we decided to sign the contract. The trainer made our workouts rigorous beating our bodies into subjection, but we enjoyed the beating in the comfort of our home. We kept our training session that Thursday evening following the doctor's appointments earlier in the day. My warmup began on the treadmill. Gods timing is always perfect. I surfed the television channels looking for a program that would help pass the time of my warmup. The Jewish Jesus broadcast with Rabbi Schneider immediately caught my attention. It was as if he was speaking directly to me when I thought I heard him say, "Stand on the word of God and don't let anything else in." I needed to hear those exact words at that very moment. I needed the promises of God to drown out all the noise attempting to cloud my mind.

Clarence Jr. and I shared the cancer diagnosis with our children after our workout that evening. The news was especially difficult for Avery to hear. She was an arm of support to a dear friend who had recently lost her mom to cancer, and now she's having to digest the diagnosis about me. But, I told her we were going to put on our big girl pants and fight! Clarence III, on the other hand, and without hesitation told me I was going to be alright. The burden of sharing the news with them was not lifted from our shoulders.

I left my goddaughter Adrienne's birthday celebration thinking and asking God that old aged question yet again, "Why?" I know nothing happens without His knowledge, but I couldn't help but ask. Before I allowed myself to go down that rabbit hole of sadness and despair, I began thinking about the promises of God. I had to encourage myself in the Lord. I had to speak healing over my body once again and not let anything else in. As I drove, I ended up right around the corner from the Costco's Wholesale Warehouse. The sweet halo tangerines I ate in abundance at the party were purchased there, so I had to go buy some for myself. I quickly thought about how my sister friends Janice, Tonya and I would make a mad dash to Costco's while our children were in choir rehearsal. I called Janice to remind her of our shenanigans. When she picked up the phone, before I could get a good hello out of my mouth, she said, "Jaculin Jones, you are going to live a long life. You are going to live a very long life". I immediately thought she may have heard about the cancer diagnosis. She fervently prayed me through the aortic dissection and had no ear to hear about anymore sickness on me. We had a full-blown praise break over the phone in the Costco's parking lot! We began to bless the Lord and thank Him for another healing.

The full understanding of chemotherapy and radiation hadn't settled in, but I wanted the cancer out of my body. I met with Dr. Zulu who shared my options for surgery. A complete mastectomy would mean removing my entire right breast, or a lumpectomy which would mean removing just the cancerous tissue leaving my breast intact. I felt that same three second sting again just hearing about the options and the decision I would need to make. The severity of my condition hit me. But, doing nothing was not an option. After Dr. Zulu informed us of the size of cancerous tumor, we elected to have the lumpectomy.

Work, home and now balancing my health were competing priorities. Stress could no longer be a part of my life. I shared a major account with a co-worker who was leaving for another position. Her departure would have placed a heavy burden on me in a very unnecessary way. I thanked God for the timing despite the circumstances. I shared with my co-workers that I would be on leave for some time due to the cancer diagnosis. They were very sympathetic. And, it never ceases to amaze me how God places special people in your life just at the right time. I forged an immediate bond with Deborah, the newest co-worker in my department. She invited me to the little grill café across the parking lot from our office. As she shared her victory over breast cancer, with tears in her eyes, she candidly told me that I was going to be in the fight of my life. I guess by my appearance I had a very calm demeanor. But, the truth was, I really didn't know all that I would face, but I was trusting God.

Faith, Faith, Faith

The Sunday School lessons during this time and prior to the diagnosis were about faith, not just our faith in God but the faith of our God. His faithfulness was in full demonstration one Sunday morning. We didn't go to church that Sunday, which for me, in particular, was a blessing. Breathing clearly was important given my past history. I began receiving text messages about carbon monoxide detected in the sanctuary during our morning worship service. The young people along with other adults began reacting as they inhaled the odorless life-snatching fumes. They said there was a calm orderly evacuation of the church. Several members were taken to the hospital, but not one life was lost. Our whole congregation could have been wiped out but look at the power and faith of our God!!!

Mother Jimmie Jones, a mother in my church, a previous babysitter to my now adult children and just a dear friend had prayer every Sunday evening with her spirit filled sisters and her 91-year old mother. When I shared the cancer diagnosis with her, she invited me into their war room. Those women not only prayed with precision, but their words of encouragement lifted my spirit. The day before surgery I received an e-mail from Mother Jimmie's sister Pam. She said the Holy Spirit told her to tell me to put my hand on my breast and plead the blood of Jesus. I did exactly that and continued to pray, believing God for my healing.

I arrived at Kaiser's Ambulatory Surgery Center on March 22nd ready to go under the knife again. Nurse Michele completed the pre-operative preparations and asked a series of questions. She also asked who would be performing my surgery. When I told her Dr. Zulu, she said he was the best and that I was in good hands. I went to radiology a little later to have dye injected in my breast. This was necessary to determine the location of the cancerous breast tissue, and to also detect any cancer that may have traveled to my lymph nodes. When

I returned to my room, Dr. Zulu shared the steps of the procedure. He concluded the steps by asking if we could have a word of prayer. Now, that sounded right old school churchy, but I thanked God for a praying surgeon. He invited my family into my room, and as we held hands, I listened intently to his prayer. He prayed for God's presence through my journey as a breast cancer survivor and also prayed for my family that they would remain strong. Then he called on the "Great Physician" recognizing his inferiority and his reliance on God to guide his hands. There was something special about him the very first day we met, so when he sealed the prayer "In Jesus name," I knew I was in the right hands. I entered the operating room, looked around and fell asleep. It felt like only a few minutes had passed before I was out of surgery looking up at my family again!!! The surgery went well. The cancerous breast tissue and two lymph nodes were removed. A very small trace of cancer was found in one of the lymph nodes which would later be confirmed, but this part was behind me. Thank you, Jesus.

The biopsy prepared me for the indescribable post-operative pain I felt. Thank God for my family who changed my bandages, and stomached measuring and draining the fluid from my breast around the clock. I pause to celebrate my husband who is truly heaven sent. He doesn't walk on water, though I believe he'd try. But, there is none like him. He truly delivers. His love for me is intentional. He considers me over himself. His happiness is tied to my happiness. He sacrifices himself for the sake of his family. He's walked with me through the most difficult times of our lives and this time was no different. I celebrate him for his faithfulness to me and our family.

We had already made lifestyle changes as a result of the aortic dissection, but the cancer diagnosis was a game changer. It demanded deliberate changes no questions asked. When I learned that sugar potentially feeds cancer cells, I hastened to remove it from our diet. This applied to the whole family. I got rid of all the white stuff; white sugar, white potatoes, white rice, and white flour. I began a predominately plant-based organic diet and avoided all processed foods. This change didn't only involve what I ate, it also involved my thinking. We are what we eat, and we become what we think over time. I know I internalized more than I was willing to admit, and my body did not lie. I had to align my thoughts according to the way God wanted me to think. It was time to get healthy by any means necessary, and it started with my mind. I'm still working on that.

Dr. Zulu confirmed that a trace of cancer was found in one of the lymph nodes. The next course of action was to meet with the oncologist to prepare for chemotherapy treatment. Chemotherapy versus a more holistic alternative medicine became an agonizing decision to make. With limited understanding, I became concerned with the unexperienced effects of chemotherapy. My bigger concern, however, was its impact on my heart. Dr. Cooper understanding my concern, ordered a Muga Scan. This heart function test would determine if my heart could tolerate the chemotherapy. I was also made aware of the option to have the chemotherapy infused through my veins or have a medical port inserted. This meant another surgical procedure, but after understanding the benefits we moved forward with the port.

Speak Lord

The Holy Spirit woke me up early one morning to pray. It was not an emotional prayer. No tears or runny nose. I just had a desire to hear from and talk to God. He led me to pray for others who were going through their own personal crisis. After I got off my knees, I went back to bed praying for the spirit of sleep to fall on me, but I laid there thinking about the chemotherapy process. Then my mind took a shift and I began thinking about God my Healer. I thought about what I should be doing while I wait for my healing. I thought about fasting first. I know fasting brings our bodies under subjection and draws us closer to God in prayer making us more sensitive to His voice. Then I started thinking about feasting; feasting on the word of God. "Fast and Feast, The Remedy for Healing." That was it! That would be the title of the message I needed to prepare for my next class assignment. As I thought about fasting, Isaiah 58:6-8 came to mind. *"Is not this the fast that I have chosen? To loose the bands of wickedness, to undo the heavy burdens, and to let the oppressed go free and that ye break every yoke? Is it not to deal thy bread to the hungry, and that thou bring the poor that are cast out to thy house? When thou seest the naked, that thou cover him, and that thou hide not thine self from thine own flesh? Then shall thy light break forth as the morning. And thine health spring forth speedily, and thou righteousness shall go before thee, the glory of the Lord shall be thy rereward."* Fasting in this sense was not about abstaining from food, but it was about service to others and in doing so our healing would come. Feasting meant making the word of God our daily bread. These two actions were tied to my healing.

I flew to North Carolina to get away for a few days. My family wasn't thrilled of course, but I needed time to just think. And whether they wanted to admit it or not, they needed a break just as much as I did. My sister Rosemary and brother in law Milford's home in the country was the best bed, breakfast, lunch, and dinner respite anywhere. It sits on six acres of land, backs to a pond with horses to the left and right, birds that nest in the lawn and the most beautiful scenic views you ever want to see. It was the perfect medicine while I agonized over the thought of chemotherapy. Why had this become such a burden? I didn't know enough about it, but I couldn't help but think about it. I was also experiencing some unusual dizziness while I was there that I couldn't explain. I didn't get much rest, unfortunately, but the time away was good for me.

I arrived home and just as I entered my door the phone rang. It was Dr. Zulu checking to see how I was doing. It was so good to hear his voice. I told him about the dizziness I was experiencing which could have been attributed to surgery or the medication, but he advised that I take it easy and to reach out to him if the feeling persisted. We also talked about nutrition. I shared with him my concerns about chemotherapy and the desire to explore other alternative treatments. I took the liberty to investigate "The Truth About Cancer" movement, which was a literal eye-opener. Their studies placed a huge emphasis on food. It was amazing to learn how much the right foods play a big part in the healing of our bodies. What people don't know could potentially save their lives. Little information is shared about the adverse effects of conventional cancer treatment, and not enough information is shared about more natural approaches to fighting cancer. The testimonials from people who were healed from cancer through holistic regimens after other cancer treatments failed were inspiring. I took all of these things into consideration and continued to seek God's counsel for the decisions I would need to make for myself.

The Lord laid it on the heart of my Pastor's wife, my First Lady Mother Jordan, to start a night of prayer every 3rd Thursday of the month. This one particular Thursday the prayer theme was "Peace." This was not by coincidence because the decision to move forward with chemotherapy weighed heavy on me. I knew I had the support of my family no matter what decision I would make, but I couldn't make this one on my own as no decision should be. I needed to hear from God! I was also scheduled to have the medical port inserted, so a decision had to be made soon. As Sister Sharon prayed, she told the Lord that someone needed to make a decision, and she asked that He give them peace. It was as if the prayer was coming from my own lips. By the time the prayer concluded, God had given me the peace I needed to move forward with chemotherapy.

Thank You Pastor Gray

Pastor Gray was the guest speaker at our 77th church anniversary. Not only was he my former Assistant Pastor, but he was also an instructor at the Refreshing Spring Church of God in Christ Bible Institute some years ago. That Sunday I knew we were in for a treat. He admonished the congregation to exercise the fruits of the spirit, but he focused his message on faith. He seemed overstuffed and time would not permit him to finish all that was on his heart. Well, how about that following Tuesday afternoon, as I'm walking out of the Giant supermarket on Annapolis Road in Bowie, Maryland I hear someone shout "Jackyyy" from across the produce section. It was Pastor Gray!!! Giant supermarket will never be the same!!! He finished the message right there - just for me. As we carried the benediction into the parking lot, I shared with him the cancer diagnosis. He understood the impact of chemotherapy and told me to make sure every time I went in for treatment to speak Mark 16:17-18 over my body. *"And these signs will follow those who believe: In My name they will cast out demons; they will speak with new tongues; they will take up serpents; and if they drink anything deadly, it will by no means hurt them; they will lay hands on the sick, and they will recover."* That deadly thing was the chemotherapy. He poured truth into me that day and told me to apply the life of the word. I also received a text message that day from my sister friend Pam. She encouraged me to read Joshua 1:7. *"Only be strong and very courageous, that you may observe to do according to all the law which Moses My servant commanded you; do not turn from it to the right hand or to the left, that you may prosper wherever you go."* I was fortified with the word.

Today's the Day

May 5th was the first day of chemotherapy. The patients' rooms were partially open, so I had a view of the other patients receiving treatment. I noticed the look that became familiar as the effect of chemotherapy was visible in their eyes, on their heads, and in their postures. I didn't want to look like that. Thank God for my nurse Kat. She patiently explained the process, the medications and their possible side effects, and what I could anticipate during and after treatment. Her soft and gentle demeanor was comforting as she shared information to help me through the process. I must say, however, as she pushed the needle through the port in my chest a "how dare you" came over me. I felt like I was being violated, but I had to focus and remembered the Word of God. *"And these signs shall follow those who believe..."* The Word became spiritual medicine for my physical condition.

The first drug administered seemed to have no effect at all. I thought ok this is good. The second drug brought on cold-like symptoms, but no big deal. I left the facility with my family feeling pretty good. We ate at the Panera Bread after treatment that afternoon and returned home. By that evening, everything changed. My energy level dropped rapidly. I could only equate how I felt to morning sickness. I wasn't sure if I was nauseous or hungry, so I chose hungry. Eating, of course, would be a necessity and eating right was even more critical. My taste buds changed from tasting everything to tasting much of nothing, but I was determined to eat and keep every morsel of food down. I had to command myself to eat. I had to hit the reset button in my mind and think beyond how sick I was feeling.

I was literally lethargic the first week of treatment. My family administered shots to my stomach every day for seven days following the treatment. This was necessary to support my white blood cell count. I also took a blood test two days prior to the next treatment to determine if my count was high enough for the subsequent treatment. I learned from the nutritionist that my vegetables should be cooked during treatment to remove any contaminants that might compromise my immune system. So, out went salad which was about the only thing I could taste. Eating had become more challenging treatment after treatment, but I continued to make the necessary changes. Thank God at every visit I either maintained my weight or gained a pound or two.

The process of going through cancer treatment is not for the faint of heart. I knew this was especially difficult for my family to participate and to watch. Chemotherapy is harsh on the body. This treatment designed to save my life felt like it was sucking the very life out of me. But, I had to press on. I was reminded why so many people die young from illnesses. It's not that they don't believe, but It's because they often grow weary in the process. But, just like the woman with the issue of blood pressed her way to Jesus for her healing, I also had to stay in the press for mine. God didn't take the previous condition away, but He made good on His promise in the process. I had to get to Jesus and trust Him to do the same for me again.

I Saw His Glory!

Was this a vision or was I dreaming? No, it wasn't a dream. It was too real. I don't know how long it lasted, but it was real. I woke up around 2:30 a.m. which wasn't unusual. I didn't do much sleeping during this time. I made my way to the kitchen and sat to a small bowl of navy bean soup, again choosing hungry. Even to chew made me tired. By the time I finished, all I could do was lay my head on the kitchen table to rest. I listened to a Christian television program for a few minutes, made my way upstairs and got back in bed. As I started to drift off to sleep, my eyes were opened by a radiant light. I'd never seen anything so vibrant before in my life. It wasn't blinding, but the brightness filled every area of my eyes. It was full of beauty. I felt a perfect peace. I saw His silhouette. It was full of light. The outline of His hair was full of light. His torso was full of light. His arms were full of light. He extended them down from his body placing what felt like a deposit in my heart-filling every space. I was full. I was whole. I stretched my arms up to Him trying to pull down all of His goodness wanting more and more of Him. It was beautiful! "He Touched Me and O the Joy that Filled My Soul." That song was so real and so true. You can't explain the feeling when the Lord really touches you. I wasn't dreaming. It was real! I kept reaching up for Him saying, "Yes Lord, Yes Lord!" It was so pure and divine! I didn't want it to end. It was Jesus Himself in all His beauty and splendor showing His greatness to little me. Oh, how I looked forward to that glorious encounter with Him again.

I was at the start of the Winning Souls, Christian Counseling and How to Prepare a Message courses taught by Evangelist Mary Jordan. I missed a few classes due to the lumpectomy procedure, port placement and now the beginning of chemotherapy, but I was determined to finish the curriculum. These classes were food for my mind, body, soul and spirit. For whatever reason the Saturday following treatment, I felt an overwhelming sense of hopelessness. I don't know if I'd felt that level of discouragement before, but there I was.

The effects of the chemotherapy wore on my body and now my mind. I was physically and mentally weary. But, I sat at the kitchen table with my laptop and my bible, and with the little strength I had, I started preparing my message for class. I thought about "Fasting and Feasting", but I was led back to the book of Joshua which I read prior to my first chemotherapy treatment and earlier in the week. As I continued to read and study the scriptures, six hours had passed and by the time I was done, I was strengthened and encouraged. I didn't quite follow the required steps to prepare a message, but the word was food to my soul as I applied it to my condition. My spirit was revived, and that heavy burden was lifted from me. God's word really has the power to do just that.

My message was changed to "Only be Strong and Very Courageous!" This was the instruction God gave Joshua who was chosen to lead the children of Israel into the promised land. God spoke to Joshua and told him all that he would possess, but He also told him to be strong and courageous. He never gave weight to any adversary that Joshua might face. He simply told him to be strong and courageous. This message was for me. I needed the Lord's strength to get through this process and He would be my strength.

I am not My Hair, but Really?

Dying my hair that soft natural black was now out of the question. Natural was in and sporting the hereditary salt and pepper would have to be fashionable too. I learned how to install crochet braids which was my new-found hair-do. I asked God to let me keep my hair. I mean what was a little chemo going to do anyway, right? Well, the Saturday evening following my second treatment, I noticed a small salt and pepper cluster of hair sticking out from my right temple no longer attached to my head. That Sunday, as I took out the crochet braids, the hair around my edges seemed to follow. It was happening. But in my normal fashion, I rocked my naturally crinkled hair and wrapped my edges with a scarf.

When I finished preparing my message that Monday afternoon, I tackled the rest of the lifeless strands of hair on my head. With every stroke, hair was left tangled between my fingers. I didn't want to think it or speak it, but my hair was falling out. I called Avery at work and told her we needed to go shopping for wigs. In her bossy tone, she insisted that I didn't need a wig. But, this wasn't my imagination nor was it because of abuse or neglect. The side effects of the chemotherapy were happening, and even though I knew this was a possibility, nothing prepared me for that moment. The emotion that you feel is indescribable. My hair just before the diagnosis was the healthiest it had ever been and now it's making a rapid exit.

Off to "Beauty 4 You" beauty supply store. I tried on all types of wigs and finally settled on a wavy, curly unprocessed wig. I sat at the dressing table in the back of the store while Avery completed the transaction. As I sat, I saw this woman in the mirror looking terrified as tears roll down her cheeks. It was me! I couldn't mask the emotion anymore. I was overwhelmed, but Avery caught me just in time. Every now and then you need somebody to tell you to get a grip. She quickly pulled me close to her side wrapped her arms around me arresting every tear. She said, "Mom, you are cancer free!" Those firm words and her strong grip dried my tears and canceled any negative thought going on in my head. We left the store with the most expensive wig she could afford. That young lady brought me back to myself. I didn't have time to think about the chemotherapy treatment later that week nor the unprocessed wig that took on a life of its own. I focused on my assignment, and hence I delivered my message to the class in its entirety. Here it is.

"Only Be Strong and Very Courageous."

"Earlier last week I got in bed, and I told God wherever my bible opened that's what I'll read tonight. There it was Joshua 1. As I began to read, this one verse captured my full attention. This was not by coincidence as nothing in life just happens, but this word was for me, and I know it will be a blessing to you.

Joshua 1:9. *"This book of the law shall not depart out of thy mouth; but thou shalt meditate therein day and night, that thou mayest observe to do according to all that is written therein: for then thou shalt make thy way prosperous, and then thou shalt have good success."*

Joshua, the anointed successor of Moses, was chosen to lead the children of Israel into the promised land after Moses' death. Moses was initially given this assignment, but he let hard-headed rebellious unbelieving people provoke him to disobey God. Even after all the signs and wonders God performed and despite how great the children of Israel were brought out of Egypt, walked through the Red Sea on dry land in Pharaoh's hot pursuit to enslave them again, being fed with manna from on high and providing water in the desert, they still rebelled against God. In God's displeasure, He determined that the forefathers of that generation would not inherit the promised land. Numbers 32: 11-13 gives you the history in a nutshell. *"Surely none of the men that came up out of Egypt, from twenty years old and upward, shall see the land which I swore unto Abraham, unto Isaac, and unto Jacob; because they have not wholly followed me. Save Caleb the son of Jephunneh the Kenezite, and Joshua the son of Nun: for they have wholly followed the LORD. And the Lord's anger was kindled against Israel, and he made them wander in the wilderness forty years until all the generation that had done evil in the sight of the LORD was consumed."* That included Moses who also died without crossing into the promised land.

Joshua's preparation to lead the children of Israel to the promised land began under the leadership of Moses. He followed the instructions of Moses and was fearless in his pursuits. Deuteronomy 34:9 says, *"And Joshua the son of Nun was full of the spirit of wisdom; for Moses had laid his hands upon him: and the children of Israel hearkened unto him and did as the LORD commanded Moses."* Joshua and Caleb were the two men that, after spying out the land, returned and delivered a good report and the assurance that they could conquer the land. He remained hopeful despite the people who were full of fear and disobedient. Even after all God had done for them, they thought they'd be better off returning to Egypt. The murmuring, complaining, and disobedience caused the mothers and fathers of that generation to die in the wilderness, but Joshua pleased God. This abbreviated history is where we find ourselves in the text, and the subject for my message, "Only Be Strong and Very Courageous."

There are three key points I want to leave with you. Be strong, be of good courage and meditate on the word of God.

I want to first focus on the Lord's instruction to Joshua because it is essential to understand the necessity of being strong, having courage and meditating on the word of God. God is now speaking directly to Joshua. No doubt Joshua spent time studying Moses. He knew the challenges Moses encountered while leading the children of Israel. Just as Moses knew God's voice now, Joshua began to recognize and know God's voice. He followed Moses' commands, but he wholly followed God. It's important that we catch hold of the vision of our leaders. As the leader is led by God and as we follow, great things happen both corporately and individually.

What is interesting in this text is how the Lord gives instruction to Joshua. God now says to Joshua just what He said to Moses in Deuteronomy 31:2-3. *"The LORD thy God, he will go over before thee, and he will destroy these nations from before thee, and thou shalt possess them: and Joshua, he shall go over before thee, as the LORD hath said."* Moses goes on further to say to Joshua in Deuteronomy 31:7-8. *"And Moses called unto Joshua, and said unto him in the sight of all Israel, be strong and of a good courage: for thou must go with this people unto the land which the LORD hath sworn unto their fathers to give them; and thou shalt cause them to inherit it. And the LORD, he it is that doth go before thee; he will be with thee, he will not fail thee, neither forsake thee: fear not, neither be dismayed."* God now reiterates this promise to Joshua.

We often hear the term "location, location, location" in real estate when someone is looking to acquire property. In this case, God tells Joshua I'm giving you this location; this land which was promised to the children of Israel and He says it's good. It's a rich land. He tells Joshua to go over the Jordan. If we go back to Numbers 33, God instructed Moses in the same way after settling near the Jordan. He also tells him that when they go over the Jordan to drive out all of its inhabitants. God didn't ask them to co-exist with the people in the land. He said drive them out leaving no opportunity for influence by the practices of those living in the land. This land was their inheritance. The Lord also tells Joshua that every place where the sole of his foot treads He's giving it to him. God is giving Joshua open access. Where your foot lands, it's yours. He says, *"From the wilderness and this Lebanon even unto the great river, the river Euphrates, all the land of the Hittites, and unto the great sea toward the going down of the sun, shall be your coast."*

Then the Lord tells him, *"No man will be able to stand before you all the days of your life."* Apply what is being said here to your own life. I thought about no man or circumstance. God never mentions the obstacles or barriers Joshua might encounter. He simply said no man will be able to stand before you or overtake you all the days of your life. That meant lifelong victory. This was God's promise to Joshua.

He goes on to tell Joshua that He will be with him. Joshua heard it from Moses, but now God is telling Joshua directly, *"I will be with you."* Chemo is an assault not only on your body, but it also messes with your mind. I had the surgery to remove cancer, but due to the rarity of the type of breast cancer, the doctors strongly recommended the most aggressive chemotherapy and radiation therapy to diminish the possibility of a reoccurrence. As you can imagine, this is unchartered territory for me. I need God to lead me through this process. A feeling of hopelessness and despair attempted to creep in and take over, but if God be for me who can be against me? This is what I had to declare to myself. If God spared my life through the last crisis, He is well able to see me through this one. As He was with Abraham, Joseph, Moses, Joshua, Jesus, Paul, He is with me. He says, "I will be with you."

Then He says, *"You shall not fail."* I can't fail in my process of healing. It's hard, but I shall not fail. He gives the assurance that failure will not and is not an option for Joshua. If God is with us, we shall not fail. He says, *"I will not forsake you."* Here God assures Joshua that He has him covered on every side. He says I'm with you, you can't fail, and I won't leave you. I had to take those promises for myself. When we have the promise that God is with us and for us, we can be the fearless people God created in His image, perfected in Jesus Christ.

Even with the promises God gave Joshua, He tells him to be strong. What does it mean to be strong? I found several definitions like "the power to move heavy weights or perform other physically demanding tasks, to be secure, well built, indestructible, able to withstand great force or pressure." After all of the promises, He tells him to be strong. But why? It sounds like a life of sweat less victory, right? Well, God knows all things. He knew that resistance and opposition would confront Joshua - coupled with doubt, unbelief, and fear. But, Joshua's job was to solely focus on the promises. He had to think as God thought. This command of strength was not only for Joshua, but it was also for the people he was leading. I was watching Dr. Mike and DeeDee Freeman Ministries one morning and the title of Dr. Mike's message that day was, "Think Like I Think." He was admonishing his congregation that they had to have the same mind. As the leader is strong, we should take on the same attribute of strength. To be strong means that we exist in strength; God's strength.

Then He says, *"Be of good courage."* What does it mean to be courageous or to have courage? There were a few definitions that spoke about doing something afraid, acting according to your beliefs or acting in the midst of pain or grief, but this one definition seemed to be the most relevant to me. It said, "The capacity to meet the anxiety which arises as one achieves freedom." Joshua strived for freedom despite the negative report from the other spies. He saw freedom despite the giants. I recall what Joyce Meyers said in one of her messages. She said, "Do it afraid." That just means to be courageous despite the fear.

Joshua is now instructed to lead this generation into the promised land and to take it over. You know it's a bold move to go into occupied territory and take over. But, in the same way God promised me good health, I needed to take courage and take hold of His truth. Jesus hung on a cross over 2000 years ago for all sickness and disease. He conquered cancer in His own body just for me, nailing it to the cross, died and rose again with all power in His hand rendering sickness powerless over me. He didn't say that we wouldn't suffer affliction, but He said in Psalm 34:19, *"Many are the afflictions of the righteous, but He delivers us out of them all."* He told me in Matthew 21:22 *"And all things whatsoever you ask in prayer, believing you shall receive."* I take courage believing the word of God and speaking good health over my body. *"I shall not die but live to declare the works of the Lord."* Psalm 118:17. *"He was wounded for my transgressions, bruised for my iniquity, the chastisement of my peace was upon Him, and with His stripes, I am healed."* Isaiah 53:5. Healing is the children's bread, and I'm His child. Paul prayed in 3 John 1:2, *"I pray above all things that we may prosper and be in health even as our souls prosper."* How does my soul prosper? My soul prospers through believing and obeying the word of God.

Then God reminds Joshua once again, *"Have not I commanded thee? Be strong and of good courage; be not afraid, neither be thou dismayed: for the LORD thy God is with thee whithersoever thou goest."* Joshua 1:9. Anything God tells you twice, any place He takes you, any trial that confronts you, any obstacle we face must be met with strength and courage knowing that God is with us. God commands us to be strong and to be of good courage. Fulfilling God's purpose for our lives requires strength and courage. He's called us to it. Having courage is having faith in God. Having faith is a matter of our lives.

How are we made strong or how are we then courageous? The Lord tells Joshua to meditate. *"Thy word is a lamp unto my feet and a light unto my path."* Psalm 119:105. He says to Joshua 1:8, *"This book of the law shall not depart out of thy mouth; but thou shalt meditate therein day and night, that thou mayest observe to do according to all that is written therein: for then thou shalt make thy way prosperous, and then thou shalt have good success."* We must feast on the word of God and be obedient to what it says. Ephesians 6:11 tells us to, *"Put on the whole armor of God, that ye may be able to stand against the wiles of the devil. For we wrestle not against flesh and blood, but against principalities, against powers, against the rulers of the darkness of this world, against spiritual wickedness in high places. Wherefore take unto you the whole armor of God, that ye may be able to withstand in the evil day, and having done all, to stand. Stand therefore, having your loins girt about with truth, and having on the breastplate of righteousness; And your feet shod with the preparation of the gospel of peace; Above all, taking the shield of faith, wherewith ye shall be able to quench all the fiery darts of the wicked. And take the helmet of salvation, and the sword of the Spirit, which is the word of God: Praying always with all prayer and supplication in the Spirit and watching thereunto with all perseverance and supplication for all saints."*

One evening I shared the news of the cancer diagnosis with my neighbor Minerva. As we talked, she told me I was in a war. She said, "Keep your sword out." I remember the late Evangelist Ezelle Howard, a prayer warrior from my church would often say, "Do the book." If we understand what the bible says and do it, we can defend our hope in God with strength and courage. His word says to, *"Trust in the Lord with all of thine heart and lean not to our own understanding. In all our ways acknowledge Him and He shall direct our paths"* Proverbs 3:5-6. Minerva and I prayed right in her driveway trusting God for my healing. What a blessing!

Joshua didn't have to seek or chase success. He didn't have the Psalms or the new testament to read, but he meditated on the holy writings and the experiences He already had with God. As he followed God's instructions, he was successful. I watched the Jewish Jesus television program one night after being diagnosed with breast cancer. Across the bottom of the screen the words read something like, "Stand on the word of God and don't let anything else in". That's what meditating means. What we go through may not be easy, but the word will speak into our situations giving us strength if we just meditate and believe. Psalm 18:28, *"For thou will light my candle (Lamp): the LORD my God will enlighten my darkness."* Those areas in my life that are dark, that I don't understand, that are troubling me, things that I need direction for, the word brings light, clarity and understanding. The word also burns up those things that war against the will of God in my life as I am obedient and as I meditate on Him.

Our acceptance of Jesus Christ gives us the assurance that He is preparing a place for us, we have an inheritance and eternal life. Jesus said He is preparing a place for those who are His that where He is, we may be also. But while we are here on earth, He's promised us territory to possess. He's promised us success. He's promised to be with us, never to leave nor forsake us. He is only instructing us while on this journey as He instructed Joshua - Only to Be Strong and Very Courageous." Amen!

I thought the weight of delivering my message was over until the instructor abruptly told the class to prepare a pop-up message to present that very evening. I was nervous all over again, but quickly drew my message from Joshua 1:8. God had already given Joshua His promises to be with him, to prosper him and never forsake him. But, after all of His promises He tells him to meditate on the word of God. God knew the obstacles Joshua would face, but He wants his attention focused on the word. For comparison, I was led to look up the word daydream. To daydream means "to have a series of pleasant thoughts that distract from the present." To meditate requires a concentrated focus on a thing without distraction. Daydreaming takes you away from the present and produces little action. But, when you meditate on the word of God it brings about the appropriate action, response and ultimate victory. Just as Joshua needed to focus, I also needed to focus on what God promised regarding my healing and not let anything else in.

Hair Gone Wild

I finished my messages that evening and the wig, well it became a backseat passenger on my way home. The next day with every gentle touch, strands of hair were left in between my fingers. That was it! The devil was no longer going to harass me about losing my hair. I scheduled an appointment with the barber to have it shaved off later that afternoon. Within seconds of hanging up the phone, my Aunt Lois was calling. She was also a recent breast cancer survivor, so she understood the process and the precautions I should take regarding my health. She quickly reminded me that a razor should not touch my scalp while undergoing chemotherapy. So, she encouraged me to cut it myself. While I had her on the phone I began cutting it down to a manageable length. I then washed the four inches left on my head. When Avery returned home, she attempted to moisturize my hair, but the moisturizer seemed to sit on the top of the lifeless strands with no penetration. I told Avery to cut it all the way down.

As I sat, I began reflecting on all the time I spent doing Avery's hair, listening to her open up to me about what was happening in her young life, things that were on her mind. Now she's a young woman doing my hair listening to me tell her about the things on my mind. When she finished my hair, she gently applied makeup to my face as I braced to see my new reveal. How I looked couldn't compare to how I felt. That moment was so precious. I asked God if I could keep my hair through the process. If He had honored my request I would have never had such a memory to cherish. I gained so much more that day. I felt loved. I felt strong. I felt courageous!

The cancerous lump that I couldn't feel was removed, but two lumps developed as a result of the surgery that I could feel. I followed up with Dr. Zulu who wasn't particularly concerned. He attributed it to the healing process but ordered a follow-up ultrasound. I remembered what came to mind that first Sunday that whatever I wanted this year I was going to have to fight for it and fight to keep it. I was in this thing to win, so I had to believe by faith that I was healed. I thanked the Lord that the test results confirmed no sign of cancer.

I was asked to join the planning committee for my church's Youth Ministry Crusade just a few weeks prior to the diagnosis. The crusade is a special time set aside every year for the children to participate and coordinate their own events and revival services. I was given the task of coordinating our student achievement awards night. God gave me the creative idea for the children to host their own talk show style awards night showcasing their academic successes and career pursuits. The event was well attended, and the children and our church congregation enjoyed learning more about the children's accomplishments and aspirations. They were going places. I also discovered that night that chemotherapy brain is a real side effect of chemotherapy. I found myself forgetting what I wanted to say and sometimes even unable to finish my sentences. But, little mattered after I spoke with Crystal that evening. She was a dear sister and a two-time breast cancer survivor. She shared her path to a holistic lifestyle and was very encouraging to me. She gave me the name of the Naturopath who helped her through her process. I didn't get an appointment with him right away, but when I did it was life-changing. He enlightened me about some of the dangers associated with conventional cancer treatment. He believed in the biblical principles of healing through the natural properties God created from the earth. Incorporating biblical principles with a regimen of healthy eating, exercise and rest would become my medicine. The journey to overall comprehensive health would require my full commitment, but positive results were inevitable if I followed the regimen.

The first round of chemotherapy did all the good and the damage it could do. My fingernails and toe nails turned black. I lost all of my hair. Dark spots appeared on my gums.

The neuropathy in my hands and feet caused burning and numbing underneath my skin. What became my biggest concern, however, was the impact on my heart. Upon learning that there was no statistical evidence to show improved results by completing the second round of chemotherapy, I discontinued the second round of treatment. Dr. Cooper recommended that I at least move forward with radiation treatment.

My first visit with the radiation oncologist was met with some concern. She was surprised and pleased to see how well I was able to extend my arm considering the short time between the surgery and my visit. I thanked God I had no issue with moving my arm on the side where the lumpectomy was performed nor any evidence of lymphedema. I only experienced numbness in my breast and under my arm which were expected side effects as a result of the surgery. Otherwise, good feeling was returning to my body following chemotherapy. The doctor shared the potential side effects of radiation and the possible risk of developing cancer from the radiation treatment. I didn't scare easy and moved forward.

I endured the pain from the tattoos administered to mark the exact position where radiation would be targeted at every treatment. But, eight days into the process, I began experiencing what felt like heart palpitations. I knew I would need to discontinue the radiation treatments and depended on God for my overall health. I met with the Naturopath during that time who developed a personalized treatment plan. It was quite extensive and overwhelming. So, I determined what I could do and went for it. The plan was working. I began to see immediate results. Food became my medicine. My body was conforming and transforming inside out. Thank you, Jesus!

It's My Birthday

My 52nd birthday would be like no other. Avery wanted to do something extra special and hosted a Yoga Birthday Bash and Brunch. It was by far the most memorable of all birthdays. Over 50 fearlessly courageous women converged upon my home to share in my celebration of life. They were there to celebrate me, but I also took the liberty to celebrate them. I wanted to let them know how much I appreciated all they had done to help me through the toughest time of my life. We started the day with a relaxing session of yoga under the sun and under the guidance of our fearless Instructor, Jade Haynes. She stretched our limbs and freed our minds. Then we transitioned to a delicious brunch and plenty of lady chatter. It was just a wonderful time to celebrate with the people who really loved me and saw me well. I was so grateful to God to have these women in my life. It takes a village.

A Spirit of Laughter

I was so excited to see another Thanksgiving Day. I totally ignored the pain in my foot attributing it to neuropathy, one of the side effects of the chemotherapy. I cooked a traditional dinner not to deprive my family of some good old down-home cooking, but I kept it as close to healthy as possible. Cauliflower mac was on the menu this year. I dressed and prepared the table for my family and invited the Pruitt family from my church. We ate, laughed, watched our team lose the football game and just enjoyed our time together. The enemy tried to rear his ugly head later that evening, but God gave us the strength to endure. We made it through another storm.

I managed the pain in my foot until Monday after work. While waiting at the pharmacy, I made the mistake of taking off my shoe in the patient waiting area. Well, when I attempted to wiggle my foot back into my shoe, the piercing pain took me straight to urgent care. The results of the x-ray revealed a hairline fracture in my left foot. Why did a spirit of laughter come over me? I couldn't help myself. I just laughed and told the devil no matter what he brings, he was not going to get the best of me. I proudly walked out of urgent care center with a medical boot on my left foot and my shoe in my right hand. I was more than a conqueror that day. I later wrote and performed a skit for our church's Christmas Cantata a few weeks later. I wrote the boot into the script. I refused to be defeated.

My follow up mammogram was December 23, 2016. You know, there comes a time in your journey that you just have to trust God for yourself and sometimes by yourself. My family didn't come with me for the exam, but nothing mattered more than when the radiologist gave me the good report. I called my family right away to let them know that I was all clear; no cancer was detected. If I didn't receive one Christmas gift that year the best gift was the confirmation of my healing. Thank you, Jesus!

Be Specific

The 2017 New Year's Revival was conducted by Prophetess Sharon Seay Whitelaw who encouraged us short of commanding us that when we pray to be specific. Her words immediately resonated with me. We often ask God to bless us, heal us, deliver us, cover us, provide for us. But, we often don't get down to the finite details of what we are asking. We make general requests and it's not that God doesn't know what we need, but He told us to ask. We often don't get specific unless we're in a crisis. More often, those are the times we find ourselves in a state of not knowing what to pray for. Well, I got a little more specific. I asked God to purify my blood and to allow His healing to run through my veins. I prayed that He would cleanse every cell in my body. I began to name my body parts. I prayed that food would become my medicine. I prayed that cancer would not have an occasion to touch my body again because He nailed sickness and disease to the cross. I prayed and reminded Him of what He did over 2000 years ago. I'm still learning how to pray beyond generalities. I prayed for my family that God would restore my son into the mighty man of God that was prophesied over his life a long time ago. I prayed that God would renew his mind, return the joy to his soul and to make him fearless. I prayed that my daughter would continue to acknowledge God in all her ways and that He would direct her paths. I prayed that her business would be a global success. I prayed that God would continue to reveal Himself to my husband and that he would continue to be the spiritual leader of our family. I prayed that we would impact the lives of the people we came in contact with as we share our story. Of course, 2017 was met with its own challenges, setbacks and losses, but God was honoring my prayer, and every set back began to propel us forward. His plan is to prosper us and to give us a future and a hope.

My brother Jody passed away in July 2017. I recalled some of the good times we had growing up. Anytime our parents left him to babysit we could count on hot dogs, baked beans, apple sauce, and salad for dinner without fail. I don't know how he put that combination together or if that was all he knew how to make, but we never went hungry. He moved away from the family when I was young and only came home on really special or unfortunate occasions which for him were few. The last time I saw him was when my mother passed away in 2007. He and I pulled out the carpentry skills we learned from our father and retiled the bathroom floor of our mother's home the week she passed away. I think that was our way of burning off some nervous energy in hopes of passing the time dreading the day of the funeral. We spoke on a few occasions after that time. Our childhood memories seemed like they occurred just the day before. My last conversation with Jody was a week before his passing. We talked about church and all the things PK's "preachers' kids" experience growing up. He spoke about the things we were taught of the Lord and what wasn't happening in the church today. I reminded him that he was the change the church needed to see, but God knew best and took him home. I believe the specific prayer mommy prayed that all of her children would be saved was honored for him.

November 3, 2017 was the day I returned for my annual exam. I continued the self-breast exams knowing the two lumps were still present. I told the technician about the lumps before the exam. I knew they would appear on the mammogram. She thought the lumps were called oil cysts but wasn't sure. I'd never heard that term before, and it wasn't for me to know until that day. She finished the exam and directed me back to the waiting area to wait for the results. Many things crossed my mind, but I didn't have time to think about the "what ifs." When the technician returned to tell me that I was good to go, I called my family thanking the Lord once again for another victory. She confirmed that there was no sign of cancer and that the lumps were indeed called oil cysts which often happens as a result of breast surgery. The Lord immediately quickened me about the anointing. He placed His anointing oil in my body healing me and leaving evidence of His healing. 2018 would be no different. #I'lltakethelumps!

Now I know

I asked God why? Why me? Why these trials? Why does God permit unfortunate things to happen in our lives? Why are there times when we waiver in our faith? How will His love and power be revealed in the earth? How will anyone know why Jesus came, died for our sins and bore all of our sicknesses and disease on the cross? I believe the answer lies in each flower's bloom. God shows His power in the earth not only through our successes and failures, but also through the trials we overcome so, *"The people you live among will see how awesome is the work that I, the Lord, will do for you. Exodus 34:10.*

As Jesus taught his disciples to pray,

Our Father
(My God)
Who are in heaven.
(You sit on Your throne)
Hallow would by Thy name.
(I honor your name)
Thy Kingdom come.
(Your Kingdom is here)
Thy will be done
(You have purpose for my life)
on earth
(right here)
as it is in heaven.
(as its already done in heaven)
Give us this day
(You load me daily with your benefits)
our Daily Bread.
(spiritually and naturally)
And forgive us our trespasses, as we forgive those who trespass against us.
(Help me to forgive others with the same grace and mercy
that you've forgiven me)
Lead us not into temptations,
(Give me the strength to endure the trials and test that come my way)
but delivers us from evil.
(be my way of escape from the evil one)
For thine is the Kingdom, the power, the glory
(You reign supreme. You are almighty. You are splendid)
forever and ever
(to the end of time)
Amen.
(And it is so!)

76

Remembering the Holy Land

I could not end this writing without sharing my journey and experience in the Holy Land. I prepared to go on this journey in 2016, which would have been the culmination of the 26-week Diploma in Ministry Development Foundation Program. The Bible history taught in class would have come off the pages. After the cancer diagnosis, treatment and recovery I knew traveling was out of the question. The next trip scheduled November 2018 would be my time to take this once in a lifetime journey. I left from Washington Baltimore International Airport (BWI) with my Pastor Bishop James E. Jordan Jr., Assistant Pastor Jimmie Moss, and other members from our church. We connected in London to meet the other travelers throughout the United States who would be joining our tour group. We were on our way!

I made it! We arrived in Amman, Jordan very early in the morning, checked into our hotel and a few hours later boarded our tour bus headed to Petra, Jordan. I immediately noticed the street signs most of which were written in Hebrew and English. We made a couple of stops visiting local merchants along the way. One salesman wrapped Bishop Jordan's head with a keffiyeh which is worn as protection from the sun. Along the drive, I couldn't help but notice how dry the desert really is. Many of the homes sat on the mountainside. The view from all around was pretty amazing.

We stopped to visit the rock believed to have been struck by Moses to quench the thirst of the children of Israel as they wondered in the desert those 40 years. This story is found in the book of Numbers chapter 20. They believe that rock continues to flow with water even today.

Welcome to Petra

The three-hour bus ride from Amman through Edom to Petra was worth the distance. Petra is known to be one of the wonders of the world. The Bedouin people living there were eager to offer horse and carriage rides through the mountain path. But, it was so amazing, I had to walk the long path to appreciate the view of the beautiful red clay mountains. Ancient carvings were visibly cut into the mountains while erosion over time created beautiful natural shapes and lines. I saw donkeys roaming the mountainside. It reminded me of when Abraham went up to sacrifice his son Isaac. We continued to walk until we approached the ancient Treasury ruins. The view all around was absolutely breathtaking. The beautiful mountains all around us were indescribable. I enjoyed my first and last time mounting a camel, but overall, this wonder of the world was a sight to see.

Welcome to Mount Nebo

The second day we headed to Mt. Nebo to visit the Memorial and the Sanctuary of Moses. Our tour guide recalled the story in the book of Numbers chapter 21 where the Hebrew people complained against God and Moses and were punished. A statue sits on top of the mountain as a continual reminder of the mercy God extended to the Hebrew people. He commanded Moses to put a snake on a pole and if the people were bitten and looked upon the snake they would be healed. The blue skies and picturesque countryside were absolutely beautiful.

Welcome to all of Israel

From Nazareth to Capernaum to Bethlehem to Jerusalem every place was steeped in biblical history. It was living history! We visited many historical sites and caves throughout Israel. We had the opportunity to see how the people lived in and outside of Old City Jerusalem. The highlight was seeing where Jesus was born and raised, taught the disciples, performed miracles, where He died, was buried and rose again. It's one thing to believe, but to experience the Holy Lands in this way was undeniable.

Herodium was a site to see. We ascended to the top of the mountain and stood on the fortress built by King Herod the Great. From the top we could see all of Jerusalem and Bethlehem. Did you know that a man moved a mountain? The mountains in Israel are enormous, but when we learned that King Herod moved a mountain to the spot where we were standing was almost unbelievable. While he had his own selfish reasons for moving the mountain, I thought if a mere man can move a mountain, we can speak to the mountains in our lives.

The Dead Sea

We visited the beautiful archeological site in Qumeran, Israel which sits on the north west shore of the Dead Sea. After viewing the site, we later peeled off our jackets and headed to the water. The temperature was warm, the sky was clear, and the water was refreshing. The Dead Sea is believed to have healing properties. I stepped in believing for healing too. I came to get everything I needed from the Lord. I noticed I didn't have one moment of pain in my left foot or my right knee the whole trip which were guaranteed areas of agitation with long walking and standing. I smuggled some of that goodness back home.

Old City Jerusalem

Old City Jerusalem was like no other place I'd ever been. We learned about the living quarters where Christians, Jews, Muslims and Armenians live harmoniously. We entered through the Lions Gate. There was police presence, but the merchants, residents and tourists walked about with no issues from our observation. It was very busy place, yet seemingly very peaceful. You could feel the change in atmosphere as we walked through the different areas. We stopped at the stations along the Via Dolorosa. As we walked, I tried to imagine what it was really like for Jesus as He walked his way through the crowds on "The Way of the Cross."

Church of the Nativity

We visited the Church of the Nativity which was a sight to behold. Hundreds upon hundreds of people waited in line to tour the church where it's believed to be the site where Jesus was born. It was worth the wait.

Church of St. Anne

I was blessed with the opportunity to direct our tour group choir in song at the Church of St. Anne in Jerusalem. The acoustics in the church is like no other. After we finished singing, I was compelled to belt out "Great is Thy Faithfulness." That moment could not have been more precious than when an Asian woman from another tour group waiting to sing joined me in song. She sang it the way she felt it, but we were in perfect harmony in the spirit. It was beautiful. It felt like heaven on earth. I thought about what heaven will be like when all of God's children really get together. What an unforgettable moment!

The Wailing Wall

The Wailing Wall was amazing! People from around the world came to place their prayer requests in the cracks of the wall. The wall was divided in two parts, the men on one side and the women on the other side. Some had their faces literally to the wall wailing and crying out to their God. I placed the written prayers for myself and my co-workers in whatever empty crack I could find. There was such reverence in that place. We didn't take pictures there. We also visited the Mount of Beatitudes, and the Church of the Pater Noster on Mt. Olive where the Lord's Prayer is inscribed in 174 languages.

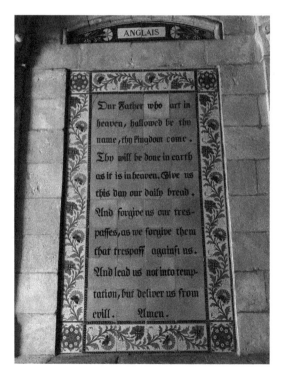

Garden of Gethsemane

    The Garden of Gethsemane on the Mt. of Olives was a sight to see. The Church of all Nations stood next to the garden believed to be where Jesus prayed before going to the cross. The garden contained age-old olive trees, some believed to be over three thousand years old. We also saw a tree of thorns believed to be the same type of thorns used to make the crown of thorns placed on Jesus head at the time of the crucifixion.

Megiddo

The Mt. of Megiddo is believed to be the site of Armageddon, the last battle between good and evil. The view from the mountain was spectacular. We also walked 183 steps down into the ancient water tunnels built by King Ahab. This historical site was as interesting as it was beautiful.

Between Two Worlds

Two time periods seemed to collide in both Jordan and Israel. The culture and religious customs dictated the way of life for the people.

The Garden Tomb

There were so many "wow" moments, one of which was during our visit to the Garden Tomb. Thousands upon thousands of people came to see Jesus' tomb and to show their gratitude and respect. We had a short communion service in the garden after visiting the tomb. The spirit of joy and gladness overcame me. I made it! I was there! Jesus came to not just save me to eternal life, but He also spared my life to enjoy this awesome experience. I shared my testimony of the journey it took to get there. The gravity of all I'd been through was worth it all.

On the Sea of Galilee

The view all around while in the middle of the Sea of Galilee was simply breathtaking. There are no other words to describe its beauty. You might imagine being on a boat swaying side to side from the waves, but it was as if we were standing on solid ground. I thought about how Jesus calmed the sea. The water was so peaceful. Assistant Pastor Moss spoke a sobering message during our service on the boat. He said we're blessed, to be broken and given. We are the body of Christ. The purpose of our lives is to be His witnesses in the earth. He said in purpose is what God chose for us before the foundation of the world and on purpose is what we do that affects us in purpose. In purpose is God's plan for our lives. If we stay in purpose, we will have favor with God and man.

We enjoyed real fresh water fish for lunch caught directly from the Sea of Galilee. After lunch, we headed to Capernaum, "The town of Jesus". The culmination of the day was being baptized in the "chilly" Jordan River. We changed into our baptismal clothing and joined other tourists who were also there to be baptized. The white doves flew above the water reminding me of when the Holy Spirit descended on Jesus like a dove. This personal experience was one of the most memorable moments of my journey.

The Grave Sites

There were no flowers; just slabs of brick and stones at every grave site. Those who came to pay respect to their loved ones brought stones to denote their visitation. The more stones, the more visitors.

The Poor will Always be with Us

Jesus said the poor would always be with us. We observed both the young and old with their cups out. A little boy standing outside of Shepherds Field offered to let us take pictures of him with his sheep for money. I observed that Israel is as rich as it is poor.

Caesarea

We enjoyed the scenic views and ancient ruins of Caesarea. This city was the creation of King Herod the Great whose vision was to build a harbor as a safe haven for merchant ships. Caesarea has a rich history. We also enjoyed looking at the crashing waters which were simply amazing.

The Land

The flowers are picture perfect. Their natural colors are vibrant and rich. As we traveled through the desert, we also came upon olive tree groves and fruit trees. How do things really grow in the dry desert? I can ask the same question about us and now I know.

114

Promises through the Journey

Romans 15:4. *"Such things were written in the Scriptures long ago to teach us. And the Scriptures give us hope and encouragement as we wait patiently for God's promises to be fulfilled."*

Psalm 32.7. *"Thou art my hiding place; thou shalt preserve me from trouble; thou shalt compass me about with songs of deliverance. Selah."*

Psalm 118:17. *"I shall not die but live to declare the works of the Lord.".*

Isaiah 53:5. *"He was wounded for our transgressions, bruised for our iniquity.*

The chastisement of our peace was upon Him and with His stripes we were healed."

Philippians 4:6-7. *"Be anxious about nothing, but in everything, by prayer and supplication with thanksgiving, let your requests be made known to God. And the peace of God, which surpasses all understanding, will guard your hearts and your minds in Christ Jesus.*

James 4:7. *"Submit to God, Resist the devil and he will flee from you".*

Mark 16:17-18. *"And these signs will follow those who believe: In My name they will cast out demons; they will speak with new tongues; they will take up serpents; and if they drink anything deadly, it will by no means hurt them; they will lay hands on the sick, and they will recover."*

Joshua 1:9. *"This book of the law shall not depart out of thy mouth; but thou shalt meditate therein day and night, that thou mayest observe to do according to all that is written therein: for then thou shalt make thy way prosperous, and then thou shalt have good success."*

Psalm 34:19, *"Many are the afflictions of the righteous, but He delivers us out of them all."*

Mathews 21:22. *"And all things whatsoever you ask in prayer, believing you shall receive."*

Joshua 1: Be strong and of good courage, be not afraid, neither be thou dismayed for the Lord thy God is with thee whithersoever thou goest.

CPSIA information can be obtained
at www.ICGtesting.com
Printed in the USA
BVHW021625010719
552380BV00013B/221/P